Endorsement: From Dr. Christine Page

From her early childhood meeting with the lady in blue, Elaine Thompson knew that she had a special gift; to be able to communicate with those from other star systems, known colloquially as ETs. From her meetings with those from Sirius, the Pleiades and many other intelligent cultures, she offers the reader fascinating insights into subjects which include inter-dimensional awareness, energy transfer and the way the human race is viewed. This book is a must for those who are ready to acknowledge our place within the Galaxy.

This book is dedicated with
All my Love
To my children, Elly and James.
I know that this World they live in will grow
even more wondrous as time passes.
I trust absolutely that they will one day soon be by my side
to meet my Extra-Terrestrial friends.

A Bright Star Press Book
United Kingdom 2000

To Andromeda and Beyond
A Bright Star Press Book
First Edition November 2007

ISBN:1-4392-1834-X
ISBN-13:9781439218341

Table of Contents

To Andromeda and Beyond. ©
Elaine J Thompson.

Chapter 1.

What does our future hold?

After pouring out the story of my life and its strange events in my first book 'Voices from our Galaxy' given to me by my Extraterrestrial friends, I felt kind of empty for a long while. The ET's were always there of course, although probably busy with their own lives, as I was. But once connected to them, that link is there for all eternity.

I spent time trying to organise my life, going through the continual process of changing, changing, and more changing. I walked away from my relationship, and found solace in the peace and quiet of my own company for three years, moving only out of my seclusion to travel.

I decided that what I *really* wanted was to be free from every kind of mortgage, bill, commitment and direct debit, and so I wrote to my dearest friend Joan Ocean in Hawaii, put all my belongings in store, and got on a plane.

The tranquility and energy of the Islands is unsurpassable, and at 2000 ft, high in the sunshine and rain of the tropical belt, I settled into a routine of gentle love and support from my adopted American family at Sky Island ranch. The Extraterrestrial's have such a strong presence there it was easy to communicate with them on many occasions, especially during the 'Meet the Andromedans' seminars and at night in the quiet energy of the star studded night.

I decided to answer the call of the ET's again, as they were telling me that there was so much more information to pass on to the world. So I began by asking a friend of mine to sit with me whilst I communicated telepathically with the Andromedan family I know so well.

Once back in England, I contacted my friend who said that he would act as the receiver of their messages. Once again, I did the sessions in Glastonbury, as the energy there is high and active.

First Session from The Andromedans:
Ptplec, son of Mir, tells of the Earth's future.

I have welcomed all my spirit guides from the earth realms, and they are standing in a circle around me. I call one of my guides a 'Light Being' but she is actually an Extra-terrestrial. She is standing with her hands on the shoulders of the friend who is sitting with me. Significantly, the Andromedan female, Mir, has brought her two children with her, and my Extra Terrestrial friends from Lyra, Sirius and Arcturus have arrived too.

The young Andromedan male (her son) has come forward. His name is Ptplec, and looks to be about 15 in our Earth years, but I know he is at least 50 Earth years old. He's carrying a ball in his hands.

His energy is bright and clear, and his telepathic communication is in tune with mine to the point of being natural, 'modern' and easy. I am now receiving both visual and telepathic information from him.

He says: Here I hold a ball in my hand. Metaphorically speaking, this is Earth; it's like a toy that has been left in a quiet corner of the Galactic Garden for many years.

Over many millennia, elements such as rain and sun have played a part in the growth of organisms all over the ball. Now is the time when it begins to bloom, and we are here to harvest (metaphorically) the best flowers.

All intelligent races from your Galaxy are now turning their attention to Earth and taking a closer look.

He asks if I understand this metaphor and adds:

We, the Andromedans, are prepared for this event (the coming of age for Earth) and now is the time to really make ourselves known to all humans that will receive us.

In the near future, people will automatically be drawn to certain locations and significant 'sacred' sites on Earth where the energetic vibrations are high. These sites are all over the globe, and will include such places as Hawaii, Sedona, Glastonbury in the UK, and many more. I mention Glastonbury because you(Elaine) know of it.

Depending on their (the people) readiness to let go of fear and allow trust in the flow of events, those who are ready can and will come with us, and will experience the lightness of being that can be felt on our ships.

Metaphorically speaking, those who will come are like the flowers on the ball (Earth), and this means we will leave people who are like the 'plant and the roots' to stimulate more growth and understanding in others on Earth. To put it simply, those people who are really emotionally ready will come with us and be taken to experience Andromedan starships and other places.

This option is not exclusive to those individuals with whom we have visited and interacted before; other people who are new to us will choose to come and visit our ships from Andromeda because they will know intuitively that all will be well.

I ask when? And the date 2014 is given to me. This is a quite a time into the future, (it's now July 2007) so what happens on earth before then?

Ptplec says: 'Between now and 2010 there will be many more contacts between us and humans, with preparation for these events as the focus. You will find that people who have knowledge of what is about to happen will find each other and get together physically.

So between now and 2010, the majority of people who are ready will spend time discovering how to step outside of the illusory realities you currently subscribe to, and will come to understand the way to leave them behind.People of planet Earth, you are all in mid-stride of a revolutionary change in your way of thinking.

The pace of this change will be rapid. If you consider the mental leap people took into the free thinking of the 60's; and then the progress on to the focus on personal power today, you will be aware of the speed of this evolutionary path you are on. The same degree of change that happened then will be achieved now in a much shorter time.

I know that you (Elaine) have been recently learning about the meaning of the Mayan Calendar, so you will understand when you witness a consciousness movement away from 'logic' into open linear/ spatial 'right brain' thinking.

Within the next five years people on earth will advance much closer to being an intuitive based society, and this brings with it the ability for people to affect their own reality. This has always been there as a possibility, but was not realised before. Those people who are closer to the land and live in more simple circumstances than those in the western world of high tech and consumerism will make this transition from logic into linear/spatial right brain thinking more easily, as this is the way they have traditionally operated within their societies—more from a creative way of thinking.

Elaine: I can understand how it must be difficult for all of you who have financial commitments and have been educated to believe that hard work equals money, and following your heart is for fools who never amount to much, because that's what I was taught as I grew up. Trusting that it will all work is the hardest thing. I found out by personal experience that only when you are in a position of having nothing or next to nothing, can you realise you have no alternative but to trust and listen to your inner feelings. Look beyond the logical stuff and see what else there is.

Wasn't it Einstein who said something like: when all possibilities have been eliminated then what is impossible must be true? This applies to reasons why we feel we can't do things, or that they are impossible. Just because you think YOU can't do it, doesn't mean it can't be done. We see good examples all over the planet of people who seem to be very 'lucky' or do the impossible…..and the Andromedans tell us that what one can do, all can do. It's just a matter of changing the way you think. Some people don't even know how to change, and are so gripped by the fear of change that they just get angry or ill when change is presented to them.

Ptplec goes on to say: You will all eventually have right brain dominant thinking. This means that you will use your abilities of feeling and intuition more. Those not into the western world of high tech and finance, those who still live in small villages and grow their own food…they have to use the intuitive side of their thinking more as it serves them better. They will find the transition much more fluid.

In contrast, in Western society where there is a greater attachment to money and material things, people will find it harder to change their views on creating their own reality, and there will be confusion and resistance. People will not understand how any kind of change will be possible.

The change is really all about people being responsible for themselves and the situations they are in, allowing for the fact that they can change their reality at any time; and letting go of fear and concern as to exactly how things can work.

There is an upsurge in the recognition of the law of attraction, and this will work well for you if you allow it. You are all so powerful, and do not realise that your thoughts create all that is around you. Simply by changing those thoughts and acting upon them, you will construct your new circumstances faster than you could have ever imagined.

Elaine: I am now being shown a great wave which engulfs the coast line of Britain from Cornwall traveling up the coast past Devon and on between Wales and Ireland. It is like the kind of tidal wave or tsunami that has been experienced in the U.S.A.

I have never seen this kind of thing in Britain before. I can see that if this happens, it could turn the focus of the British people toward helping each other and will unify them. I feel that this may happen within the next 5 years, between now and 2012. The wave comes in and thankfully goes out again, like a Tsunami, and I see that this will not only happen in the U.K. but in other places too.

Newsflash! : November 08, 2007 Tidal Wave Poses "Extreme Danger To Life."

> 1300 hrs Pacific Time Thursday Nov 08 2007. The Daily Mail UK says an urgent alert has been issued because a tidal wave is threatening coastal areas of England and Europe.

> "A three-meter tidal surge is predicted to surge down the English Channel in the next 12 hours posing an "extreme danger to life and property", experts have warned.

> Coupled with storms and high tides, the wave could leave swathes of the east coast under water, according to the Environment Agency.

> A combination of gale force winds off the coast of Scotland and high tides are expected to cause floods which could breach sea defenses."

European forecasters today warned of high winds, extreme snowfall and avalanches.

End of newsflash.

Ptplec: I want to speak to you now about energy and methods of travel.

If you want to *really* learn about the Universe, you can begin by placing your focus of attention there. When learning about the Universe, it will help the people of Earth to identify themselves as planetary or Earth beings, rather than thinking in terms of which individual country or nation they come from.

As time goes on people will again shift perspectives until they begin to think of themselves as belonging to this Solar System, and then finally from the Milky Way Galaxy (Galactic). People will be able to identify with a much bigger picture than the limited reality you all see yourselves in now.

To come back to the metaphor of the garden where the 'ball' (Earth) lies. This garden is your Universe and is full of unlimited possibilities and endless wonders. There is enough to keep Earth beings fascinated and in awe (as we still are) forever. Imagine a bird table in this Universal 'garden', which is high up and overlooking the whole. Would it not be interesting to be lifted to the top of the bird table for a better view of your Universe? I could not think of anyone who would refuse the opportunity to take that experience, and it will all be achieved through greater awareness of the existence of life beyond your Earth.

Walking through walls using the law of attraction and intention.

Question: Will peoples awareness of all of this be 4th dimensional? That is, will they only be able to see it in the minds eye, and not with their physical eyes?

Ptplec's answer: Thank you for the question. I will explain about the 4th Dimension. In a simplified way, the 4th dimension occupies the spaces in between the molecules of the 3rd dimension. In order to be aware of it, you must shift your focus of attention, or your way of seeing things. I will try to explain a little better.

The solid matter of the 3rd dimension is visible whilst your focus is still aimed there, and forms your reality. So, instead of continually looking at the perceived reality in front of you, such as a chair or table, look with soft eyes at the edges of everything, perhaps making your eyes slightly out of focus, in much the same way that an artist might look at a tree. When any artist looks at a tree, they see both the tree shape and the negative shapes around it. They are not focusing on what they *think* a tree ought to look like, but on the shape.

This awareness of the space around the tree enables you to detach from logical thinking (this is a tree) and to achieve a perfect drawing of the tree without having focused directly on it. By changing your focus and thoughts you can achieve so much. Detach your thoughts from labeling and naming things, free yourself from learned concepts, and expand into unlimited possibilities!

When you see an object in front of you, try looking at the space about halfway between you and the object. With this simple practice, you will soon understand what I am saying and begin to be able to step towards seeing different realities. When you are ready for more, try seeing the space beyond the object, by ignoring what your brain tells you is there. You may not see into the 4th dimension by doing this, as it is just an exercise to train you to think differently. Here is another exercise for you. Look at your table, see what is on it in your third dimension. It could be a book, a cloth, or any number of items. Now look at the surface of the table as if there was nothing on it, use your imagination to visualize a clear table, or maybe no table at all! Eventually, you will be able to see everything this way, and when you can, you will realise that you can walk through walls as if they were not there, because for you, they will *not* be there as your attention will be focused on a differently reality, *and you will have changed your vibrational frequency.*

You will have equalized yourself in frequency with the spaces in between the 3rd dimensional atoms and molecules by the law of attraction and intention. You will learn that you can be anywhere you want to be, just by changing your focus of attention, and the vibration that you normally resonate at.

I often go to my home planet, simply by wanting to be there. I see myself as 'I am there' and then I am!

Question: When you change your focus of attention and travel to another place does your physical matter go with you, or is it just your energy?

Ptplec: How I travel is similar to how you all will be able to travel in the future.

In the future, you will be able to move your physical self with the help of an energy transporter. This is not so much a machine as a safe space where you change the focus of your attention. You are then able to send molecules of your energy and light to wherever destination that you are focus on, simply by the power of intention. Energy can go anywhere instantaneously. It is not like physical travel, where you might measure the distance between two places by miles or kilometers. The distance would be more like two centimeters! Your scientists are already discovering in their quantum experiments that every molecule has its twin somewhere else in the universe. The basic principle of this is that by focusing on one or the other of these twins that the shift between two 'places' is possible. What they don't know yet, is that the 'twin' can be anywhere you decide it will be.

If I have part of my energy on the ship and part at home I can move between them easily by focusing on either one, and then that reality becomes the 'real' one.

Physical molecules follow the energy to its destination. I do not materialize in the new place as some kind of a wispy representation of myself. My energy and physical matter are infinitely attracted, and when one aspect of myself goes, then the other must follow.

If I have located to my home planet, I can also focus my mind on this ship, and communicate with my mother telepathically. These abilities and the technology with which to achieve it will be with you within the next 10 years, (that is if you don't all kill each other), (he laughs). Although I joke, I know that there will minor changes in structures (buildings, cities) and locations (countries) around the planet but these Earth changes will serve as a teaching aid as indicated earlier. I must remind you here that although this technology will be here on Earth, your past history has shown that not all things are revealed to the people, and are unfortunately kept secret by the few who wish to dominate.

I have no doubt that you will all learn to adapt to the changes very quickly. Concepts of other realities and ways of being will be rapidly taken on board by many people, and this process will become natural and normal. Shifts in awareness will happen on a rapid basis, and as soon as the last has been assimilated, a new concept will appear.

For example, Newton's discovery of gravity through watching an apple fall from the tree, begged the question, why doesn't the apple just float in mid-air? This began a consciousness awakening to the 'law' of gravity. What was more important was the way it made people think about what gravity implies, and the cause and effect.

So with these rapid changes, learning and intention will accelerate at the same rate as your ability to manifest and assimilate the changes.

You will come to realise that you have the capacity to bring about major changes on Earth in an entirely different way than previously known. All that is required is an internal personal change of vision, insight, focus, reality and intention.

Earth beings will be like Galactic gardeners affecting change in the environment in your Solar system and the Milky Way Galaxy. This changing will apply not only on Earth, but on other planets too. Other races in your Galaxy are growing and changing too.

Major changes are occurring in your Solar system right now, due to changing activity of your Sun and the quadrant of the universe in which you are traveling through at present. (see Solar Rain by Mitch Battros). Apart from the Galactic spin, the entire arm of the Milky Way is on a rapidly curving trajectory, bringing Earth and your closest neighbours Venus, Mars and Jupiter into contact with other influences such as the photon belt. The Van Allen belt around the planet also has a constant influence on the Earth because of the input from your Sun and its emissions. Your scientists have not even *begun* to analyze the weather systems on Venus or the nature of that planet, or to know what is happening with the next largest influence in your solar system to the Sun, which is of course, Jupiter.

Question: Do we receive any information on this whilst we are in a sleep/dream state that might help us to prepare for all of this?

Ptplec: Yes, you are more open to receive information whilst asleep, although many people use this sleep time to review the history of this life they are in, their week or their day, simply by replaying events that have occurred and trying out different alternatives to the choices that they made.

For example: in any given event that you might be reviewing, what if you had had a rubber duck in your hand instead of an axe? What if you had said *this* instead of that? In doing this constant reviewing, some people are taking refuge in the 'television' of the mind. Consequently, they have little or no time, or any intention to receive this information from us. Others may spend their time reviewing their perceived Karmic debt from past lives and will spend time trying to account for their actions in past lives, in order to ascertain their next right action. This too is a distraction. Until these reviews are resolved there is no time allowed for receiving new information from us or any other source during your dream state.

There are those, however, that have come to terms with who they are, and are at ease with change and flow, who are able to step outside of their physical body with ease, and regularly come to us for communication. We can 'download' thoughts and concepts to many that are open to receive at the right moment in time. Their brainwaves are required to be at the optimum level (as in different levels of sleep and dreaming) and then information exchange is easy.

People at the forefront of facilitating the changes on planet earth were chosen a long time ago and come from all strata of societies. They were chosen according to their genetic predisposition and ability to communicate. Some are old friends to us, and some are relatively new.

Elaine for example came in with prior knowledge of us and selected a vehicle (body) which after genetic modification could work well with us. By the way, my mother sends greetings to you Elaine, and is glad we are working with you again. I look forward to our next communication. It has already happened and was a success.

Chapter 2.

Another planet like ours:

Eco-roads and hover cars, new polymers, and controlling the weather.

The session opens, and I am once again speaking to Ptplec from Andromeda.

Ptplec: Can you remember we were talking last week about the growth of consciousness on the planet, and we said it would be like picking flowers?

We talked about the concept of taking those who are ready and expanding their awareness even more to accommodate the knowledge of our presence in your Galaxy.

I would now like to take you to another planet to show you exactly how progress and development has worked before with races of people who were similar to Earth people in their progression. This was at a time when they were reaching a critical point with their awakening consciousness.

Elaine: I can see a planet. This planet looks initially like our moon as it seems to be grey all over, but as I am zooming in closer I can see buildings that look like skyscrapers. It is so similar to our earth, it could be Manhattan.

The landscape in front of me is similar to the Manhattan skyline, with lots and lots of concrete buildings all over it. Now I'm pulling back visually and seeing it from a distance. I can see water, the same as there is here on earth, and Ptplec is taking me into an office in one of the buildings.

I see someone in a suit, so it looks to all intents and purposes exactly like being in a corporate office on earth. What he wants to show me is how corporate business works differently on this planet.

He shows me a board meeting, a whiteboard on the wall displaying a block graph on it, and someone is speaking to a group of people saying to them: How can we balance what we are doing globally?

I have a feeling that he (the man) is talking about trees, and that his company is one that cuts down trees to produce many things such as timber for building and manufacturing goods, paper and general industry. On one wall is a complete picture of the world, flattened out like a map, and he is taking into consideration the weather patterns. He is discussing what the impact of cutting down a certain amount of trees in a particular place would be; referring to the local climate, and the type of topsoil in that area. The terminology is very much like an advanced form of our 'green ecology' at this present time on Earth.

The people there are giving top priority to the amount of oxygen that trees put into the atmosphere, and also considering the fact that they help to keep the climate and the quality of the land stable. The man in the suit says that in considering global weather patterns, the weather patterns over the sea are most important.

To give me an example, I am shown the wind currents we have on our planet that blow around the earth, such as El Niño. I am also being shown the melting glaciers on our planet, which are altering the temperature of the water. He tells the people in the board room that it's extremely important for people in industry to be very much aware of *all* aspects of what they do and the consequences.

I know that we on Earth are already aware of that problem, but are addressing it too late. The time has arrived when we are all going into a cycle of heavy Solar activity, and these influences will determine the biggest climactic changes on Earth. Pollution is another thing when it comes to our personal environment. As the wise Native American Indians once said, 'If we poison our land and water, then we are destroying our means of survival'.

Ptplec tells me that we on Earth are concentrating our efforts in the wrong quadrant, and that we should be focusing our attention much more on tree planting and weather modification technology, so that we can direct rain where there is none, and allow more sunshine by clearing the fog and the clouds in other areas.

He is insistent that we not alter the weather systems for gain or profit, but manipulate them simply to keep the big things that make a huge difference to the planet in balance. For example, the North and South poles, the glaciers, and the wind currents that travel round the earth, those are the most major factors that go towards keeping our planet's temperature balanced and stable. These need to be addressed, as we will need as much help as we can get dealing with Solar changes.

Ptplec is taking me back to the other planet now, and I can see that this civilization uses hover cars that have no need for fuel of any kind.

Elaine's thoughts: This brings me to realise that hover cars can go over any terrain, don't need tyres, and don't really need roads either......

Ptplec: What this also means, (if this were here on earth) is that you could take the barriers down from the sides of motorways, highways and autobahns. Any road that goes through fields and countryside could use the fields as they are as extra traffic lanes, without having to spend millions of pounds on putting hard surfaces all over it.

Elaine: I see a green highway made of grass on this *other* planet now. It's very short grass, and I don't know whether it needs any kind of maintenance, but having it like this takes away the need for covering the soil and the land with tarmac, concrete and similar things which cover the soil permanently.

He is also pointing out the lighting on this highway. All the roads are lit at night with a kind of blue glow which looks like 'halogen' lamps. But my feeling now is that it's not halogen, it's some kind of self-perpetuating gas that gives a blue light, so it looks almost like daylight on the roads, if you can call them roads.

He says that the civilization on this planet have come to realise the true value of having land; land that they can cultivate and farm, to intensively produce good food, such as fruit and vegetables. I also see a lot of food production done under circular geodesic domes, and these are shaped like a ball cut in half with triangular panes of 'glass'.

He is telling me that although it's not as practical space wise to have round growing domes as opposed to long rectangular greenhouses, it is more beneficial for the plants to be in a circular formation with walkways through the centre. He explains that each of the four compass points, (like on a clock) are kept open to the elements, so that there is always a current of air coming north and south east and west.

This is also good in times of storm or high wind, because if you open the doors then nothing gets destroyed or blown over, the wind just passes through, and does the minimum amount of damage.

And he's saying of course, with this civilization chemicals are no longer used. In fact, the chemical industry has found its forte in building materials, with new forms of polymers and plastics that are stronger than steel and can be made from all the waste products. On Earth, when developing something, the tendency is to try and find some way to use the waste products left over. Invariably they go into medicines and cheap forms of plastic that are toxic.

Ptplec says there are safer ways to construct things, ways in which there will be no waste materials afterwards. There will be new polymers and plastics which are very strong and can be made or turned into *anything*, such as buildings, cars, even knives and forks. The cars never rust and are virtually dent proof, and he says it's just around the corner from being discovered on our Earth.

Elaine: He also shows me clear Perspex-like or polymer case that looks like you would imagine a see-through cheese board cover would be, and he says you can store food in there so that it doesn't dry out or deteriorate, from air getting to it.

Ptplec: The discoveries that will come in the future from the chemical industry will enable you to dispose of lots of the toxic packaging that you use these days. This will be because the packaging will be almost like glass; it won't give off any fumes, or leak toxins into the environment, so it will be safe.

Elaine: He tells me that one of the biggest components of this polymer will be silicon, and I'm not sure whether he said 'blended with steel'. I can't see how it could be blended with steel......No, he corrects me and says:

Ptplec: Silicon manufactured like steel which can be pressed, rolled, cut, made into any shape, poured, joined together, and generally used for almost anything. It can be made into houses, boats, cutlery, cups, glasses, everything. With this new polymer, your mining industry will be diminished, and there won't be any need to extract so many raw materials from the Earth. Having said this, there will be *something* that you will need to take from the environment, and there is also an element within the sea that will go into the manufacture of this polymer.

I hear you ask the question, and yes, this element is known to man, but it has never been used in combination with the chemicals it needs to work with in order to fuse together properly in all its aspects. It's one of those things that will be discovered by accident, although I will say that nothing is ever by accident. When the time is right, it will appear as if it had always been there.

Ptplec: Concerning the civilization on this other planet, they also have much longer days than you do here on earth. Not because of the moons or the Sun, but because they artificially light with the blue light like daylight (mentioned before) well into the night, for example, such as midnight or two o'clock in the morning.

The people there have decided that they will split their day with six hours of work and then 12 hours of following their own pursuits. Some people are concerned with planetary things for maybe two days of the week (and I am talking to you in earth's concept of time so that you can understand), and the rest of the time they are free.

I point this out because when your civilization has advanced more, you will find that there is less need to labour, and have more time to be creative. That in itself will allow the scientists, chemists and biologists amongst you to progress even faster. The feeling and concept I want to convey strongly here is that 'less is more'. Less effort and less physical labour will achieve much more than you ever have before, simply because a lot of the systems and ways you do things will no longer be necessary.

For example: In the time of your Industrial Revolution, it may have taken a week to get coal from one part of the country to another, by barge or train. Everything needed a lot of manpower, effort and time. Although things have speeded up in some places in the world, there are still many areas that take everything by horse and cart, mule or buffalo, and even by foot. All of this hinges on your concept of money; when we have impressed the importance of 'less is more', and you realise that you can achieve things in your lifetime with more simplicity, you can then put your energy and attention to what is much more globally important. Once realised, you will be able to see the bigger picture I try to illustrate.

Elaine: Ptplec is trying to give me the whole concept of what it will or could be like with no monetary system. Hardly any labour, more use of telepathy: more self-creativeness, more leisure time, more thinking time. More expansion of the mind time, less quantity but better quality of food; things that grow faster and are more nutritious, and an explosion out of the work and slog mentality and into the creational mentality. And within that, you can still create the all the things you need to survive for the love of it, and without all the trappings and frippery that we have now.

Ptplec: The most important things that have emerged on the other planet I showed you is their ability to travel differently around their planet and into their seas; plus the ability to do that without harming the environment *in any way*; their ability to create things of beauty and inspirational works of art; the ability to use their minds as never before, with telepathy and in communication.

Then what came to them after the ability to travel anywhere they wanted on the planet, is the desire and the progression towards traveling out from their earth into the solar system, and from then out into the Galaxy. There needs to be many steps taken before you on Earth get to that stage; firstly to make it possible, then to make it easy, and finally to make it safe. So before you can step on that progressive ladder you need to be in the same kind of mode or format that I have just shown to you on the other planet where so much has changed. Then you will be ready for the kind of technology that takes you from here to Andromeda or anywhere, in the blink of an eye. As you are now, you could not or would not accept it, could not cope with it physically, and it is just not possible….. or let's say, it is possible, but not practical right now, but it will come in the future.

The end of fighting and the beginning of co-operation.

Question: This seems to intimate the end of commercial competition and the blossoming of co-operation. Can we be sure of how this transition could take place?

Ptplec: Without co-operation there is destruction. Without co-operation, there is always separation, and unfortunately, in simple terms what's happening on your planet right now is complete separation and polarisation of left brain-right brain thinking.

Your thinking varies from 'there is only one way' to 'there are many ways', and to illustrate this, it is like looking at two ends of the same stick. The people of your planet have to really understand the nature of their differences, and in acknowledging the nature of their differences, they can then search for their similarities.

I just explained to you about man's need to labour and the need for money, which are logical things to you right now –for example, you have to dig something up to get it out of the ground, you have to pay money if you want to buy it because those who 'own' the land say 'it's mine'.

Once this way of doing things is gone from your society then co-operation and bargaining will be much easier. But at the moment, that's like asking which comes first, the chicken or the egg?

Unfortunately, as long as you have polarisation of belief, such as one faction saying what's mine is mine, and if you don't think like I do, then I'm going to kill you. Then the other faction on earth which says, 'we are all here on this earth and we need to be brothers in the light, we need to be all dealing with global warming, and all giving food and assistance to each other. Of course there are many shades of grey in between, but the important thing to know is that both of these elements are growing stronger.

This means that the elements that are self-involved and negative will change or self-destruct. This is because, simply by the law of attraction, and our 'cosmic laws', there is no future for any species which will not adapt and change. These species who will not change eventually die out, because only those which adapt and change to preserve their environment, flow with others needs being met, and care for peoples survival will flourish, because it can't be any other way.

You will find that there will be a huge sense of cooperation between those people who are willing to change, simply because they need to survive and without freely sharing their knowledge, you will still have separate elements.

I must also mention that although some people on your planet may feel that the internet is a curse, it's actually the route towards openly sharing everything with everyone. Because of this you will find even now, (unseen by the governments) that people are changing; cooperating and collaborating with one another, and they are the ones that will survive the natural changes and implement the changes in the way the world functions.

You will also find that self-destruction comes a lot quicker to those who are not prepared to change, now that this exponential curve is in motion. As with all things that are in motion, progress gets faster and faster until one day there will be no more fight left in anyone, and they will be glad to be peaceful. Those people who wish for peace now and those people who wish to share and co-operate will spill over and influence those that are left that want to fight, and the affect will be so compelling that the last remaining ones will change.

I speak about all factions around the world that fight one another simply because they believe that others should be like them or that others are not as good as them. It is all about possessions, power, or beliefs. Does that answer your question?

Next Question: Yes. I am also very interested in the transition with those business people on the other planet. Will there be pioneers here on Earth who will help people to suddenly switch perception?

Ptplec: Yes, help will come from many areas. Some people who are already involved in business now will make their own transition through life changing events, illnesses, or personal circumstances. The flow towards this is unstoppable, and you can compare it with the switch towards eating more organic food, and becoming healthy by being aware of the quality and quantity of what you eat. In earth terms, it will be a case of change, or your business fails.

With those that have their children inherit their business, the change will come more rapidly with the children. It is very difficult to see the scale of change that is already happening now, as it is impossible for you to see the whole picture worldwide. The majority of ordinary people don't always have their attention focused on it, but it is happening now.

For example, I pull from Elaine's mind the story of Henry Ford, who had the biggest impact on America with the manufacture of his cars. Finally his son has taken over the business, and the first thing he wanted to introduce was a hydrogen powered car, and is now producing them. It is said that he has lost lots of money, but still he continues, because he knows where the future is going. Those who inherit from him such as his children or the people he has working for him, will see the future. They will see that there is an end to oil, petrol, and fossil fuels and change has to be made. So, the band of people between 20 and 50 in age are the ones who are making the changes right now.

They are the ones who are influencing changes into school systems, industry, commerce, into every area imaginable. It's just not always visible unless you look for it. It is like a flower just below the surface of the earth, waiting to emerge and bring forth leaves and flowers. The most important part is the root-which is now- where the life force and the growth are.

The power structure that you have on the Earth is fighting its last fight to keep the eyes of the people blindfolded so that they don't see that this change is happening right now. Remember that the things you talk about spiritually are spoken about all over the globe by millions and billions of people. The momentum of change is gathering strength and will finally overwhelm and become a stronger voice to be heard over those who are in power now.

Elaine: This is interesting; he has gone right off this subject for a moment. He is holding out his hand, and asking me did I know that there is a fruit here on our planet which contains almost everything you need to survive?

I see it, and its a little round fruit, like a small crabapple or large rosehip, with little bits on the end like an apple; it's small, about the size of large grape; it's round and the colour is somewhere between red and purple, plum coloured possibly.

Elaine: Where does it grow?

Ptplec: It grows almost everywhere.

Elaine: Okay, so does it grow in cold climates as well as hot climates?

Ptplec: No, it can grow in the wild anywhere that is a fairly temperate zone.

Elaine: I am not sure what it is, I could look it up; it could be medlar or guava, as it looks similar to that.

Ptplec: I am very concerned that you remember and write down everything that has happened here, in order that is not forgotten. I have held back on a lot of important information, because everything I give you needs to be digested and remembered before we can really start to expand on other concepts. We will now go back to the other planet, and I will show you the hover principle for sea craft and boats.

Anti Gravity and neutralizing nuclear waste.

Elaine: I now see that this drive principle is not like our hovercraft at all. I immediately thought of 100 foot waves and storms at sea, and thought, 'how could a hover boat survive out in that?

Ptplec: No, you are not understanding this yet. This sea craft can hover over the top of water, and can also fly a hundred feet above the water. So if there was a storm it could fly back to shore or go up above the storm into the clouds. It has all kinds of capabilities that have nothing to do with what you would call a hovercraft. It is like a little space craft, and it can really do much more than that.

Elaine: I see it, and there doesn't seem to be anything underneath, like the skirt you would see on a hovercraft. But I see that there is some sort of field that makes it come up off the ground. I bet it has an antigravity device.

Yes, I'm told it's an anti-gravity device, so it's not using air pressure to lift itself off the Earth, its using antigravity. It has omnidirectional thrust; up, down, and sideways, and enough power to go anywhere you could want to go. With a vehicle like that, (if it was strong enough, which I assume it is), you could go under the water as well, because I believe the safest place in a storm is under the water.

Elaine: Wow, this is interesting! It's amazing you know, just before Ptplec goes he is showing me how you could make a house from the polymer resin he described, and instead of having to dig huge foundations, you have four extended poles, one on each corner. They go a long way straight down so that they lock into the earth, to ensure that the structure doesn't blow away in strong winds. Also, if you wanted to make the polymer look like old stone you could; you could make it look like anything you want.

Question: What about the amount of energy that is needed to manufacture this polymer. Will we still have a need for nuclear power?

Ptplec: In the interim, yes, whilst forms of energy you use now are being phased out, but not in the absolute future. You will eventually have advanced technology and will have no need for nuclear fuel. When we come to interact more fully and begin to teach you, we will show you how to neutralise nuclear waste. Nuclear power will be a thing of the past, because in truth it is far too dangerous and polluting to be used in the form it is in at the moment.

There is a key element about nuclear fuel that you haven't discovered yet, that can be modified and changed into something that is usable. It has to do with the molecular structure of uranium and plutonium and the way that they are used. They need to be altered slightly in order to be able to put them to a different use. We can neutralise radioactivity for your benefit, as the form it's in now is far too unstable and potentially lethal to be used.

Chapter 3.

Concerning our Sun and its affect on Earth.

Well, my guides and ET friends are all here again today, but I am not quite sure what we are going to talk about. The Andromedan male Ptplec has come forward and has started off by showing me a volcano.

I thought that perhaps we were going to talk about weather patterns on the Earth again, but from seeing the magma erupting from out of the volcano, he then took me out into space to view the Sun. He speaks:

Ptplec: Have you ever wondered what happened to all the debris that gets spewed out from your Sun all the time? The atmosphere around the Sun is of course not the same as that which you have on earth.

When there is a huge explosion of flame, gas and material, (M or X class flare, as you call it) the debris doesn't all fall back to the planet's surface. A lot of what is ejected is drawn out into space, and it fills (what you call) the vacuum of space with tiny particles of metals, ores, chemicals and higher frequency rays. Those particles from the Sun, (i.e. parts of the body of the sun), or to put it another way, from the internal mass of the Sun, are spreading out through space, and huge amounts land on planet Earth.

We, and your scientists talk in terms of solar rays, gamma rays and solar wind, but your scientists seldom take the right kind of samples from Earth's soil and the atmosphere to determine *exactly* what it is that the Sun is throwing at your planet. A lot of these particles have a huge influence on the way you all think and feel.

Your astrologers using age-old systems have calculated certain 'types' or trends in people; (for example people who were born in certain months of the year are under a particular sign). These are true findings, simply because the planets *do* influence you all by frequency, depending on their various positions relative to earth at different times of the year. But there is also the added influence of physical solar activity.

Our ships have shields around them to protect us from the vast fluctuations of matter and frequencies from different clouds of gas and toxic substances (toxic to us that is), that come from the Sun, but you on Earth have to put up with whatever gets rained down upon you.

Elaine: I ask him why is he telling me this, and what relevance does it have to right now?

Ptplec: There is likely to be vastly increased solar activity over the next 50 years. If you look to your records of solar activity, already there has been a marked difference in the way the Sun has been behaving over the last four or five years. If you remember, I was talking to you about the spiral arm of the Milky Way in which your solar system is contained; I spoke to you about it curving through space. The whole Galaxy, including of course the arms of the Milky Way is slowly turning and moving through space and always encountering different chemicals and elements, such as you will find in the Van Allen Belt around Earth and the Photon Belt you are moving into.

But also remember that your Sun and *all the other planets* in the solar system are also passing through this quadrant of space, and all feeling the effects too.

Your Sun, which is a burning mass, is affected by everything around it. You call this 'the vacuum of space', but really the atmosphere or space around the Sun is teeming with energy and particles.

On Earth, if you allow more oxygen into a fire it burns more brightly, or if you were to put some other chemical on the fire, like magnesium or sulfur, it would burn blue or yellow, and burn more intensely. If you deprive fire of oxygen, the flame goes out. So really I have to warn you that there are likely to be some **huge** changes in the way your Sun behaves over the next 50 years.

I am not saying that you won't still have Sunlight, because you will. But (going back to weather patterns) because the Sun influences the weather patterns on Earth tremendously, you are likely to be in for a period of intense heat. With this increased intensity of heat, what you call global warming will speed up, and you will have dramatic extremes with rain, storms, wind and sudden climate changes. I can say that it is 10% to do with what you are doing (the pollution) on the earth, and 90% to do with the natural cycles of the solar system and your Sun.

So there is coming a point in time when things will be very different on Earth. The temperature and the climate will be changed, the waters will rise, and there is a very strong indication that both the North and South Poles of Earth (and other planets in your system) will melt completely and will not refreeze. This being the case, there will be a huge rise of the waters all over the earth. But although having said that, there is a small percent of chance variability which will mean that the South Pole may retain some ice.

Some things you can be very sure of; the Sun is moving through a different quadrant in space and will react to the chemicals there; you will have a lot more solar activity, and therefore the weather conditions on this planet will be quite extreme, resulting in many more violent storms, earthquakes, high winds, earthquake and volcanic activity.

I was listening to you speaking (Elaine) about America earlier today.

I fear that such a large continent (especially in its global position) will be subject to (in your words) a battering from the elements, to a degree that has not been experienced before in recorded history. So whilst it will still be okay to travel to the American continent, it is extremely important that you stay in touch with your intuition, and always err on the side of caution with your travel plans. You will be able to circumvent difficulties; for example if a coast is affected, you will be able to fly around or fly beyond and find some other airport to land on, but conditions will not be easy in America, and that is putting it mildly.

There will also be other countries which will be affected, including the west coast of Africa, the Azores Islands and Tenerife in the Canary Islands, as well as the islands on the Asiatic side, Japan and the smaller islands beyond; New Zealand to Hawaii. Now more than ever, it is important to prepare cultivation on any land you may have. With this I mean for you all to cultivate your gardens, get accustomed to growing things for yourself, and take advantage of the increased sunshine that is on its way. In the in the future you will be able to grow many more tropical things here (in England) such as bananas, avocados. You must get used to it; it will be a needed element to counterbalance the structure of civilization's whole reliance on money, and the difficulties you have with pollution through the vast amounts of waste you generate.

Self sufficiency as a way of life, supplementing what is available, is something that will come back to you in the future. Many of your people used to have large gardens or an allotment of land in the past, and now even more, land needs to be used properly to support people.

Planet Miras and the 'fish' people.

Elaine: He has now changed tack completely, and he is taking me to a planet he calls MIRAS, and all I can see is water on the surface of this planet, I assume there must be some land somewhere, but it is not a lot, maybe small continents rising on a planet that is three quarters covered in water.

I can see domed buildings free floating on the surface of the water, and they move and sway from side to side.

Question from Elaine: If there is land, why do they build the domes on the water?

Ptplec: Yes, there is land, but because there is so much water, the beings here thought, 'why not use the space on top of the water?

Elaine: What happens to the domes when there is bad weather?

Ptplec: The domes can rise up from the surface of the water if it gets too rough.

Elaine: I see a small dome where people live, and it looks really beautiful. The people anchor the domes fairly close to the shore, so that they can swim and do many things underwater as well as above.

Question: Why don't they build domes under the water?

Ptplec: People need the sunlight. The refracted light that you get underwater is not enough to sustain the human system. You need to be up in the light.

Question to Elaine: Can you see any people there in the dome?

Elaine: Yes, there are human forms there; I can actually see someone diving off of one of the platforms around the dome into the water. They look to be pretty much humanoid with two arms and two legs, and they are very tall, much taller and slimmer than we generally are. I can see the back of someone as they are diving into the water, and this feels like a female.

There is something that she is wearing on her head, which I will try to describe: If the person was upright it would be very smooth on the top of the head, but at the back, where someone's hair would hang down, there are lots of slim metal rods with tiny balls on the ends of each one. They are not joined solidly at the root, so not stiff but very flexible and movable. So when this person dives into the water, the rods stream out behind her (I have absolutely no clue what that it is), and when she is under the water the rods float upwards and outwards, a bit like a sea urchin with its spines extended.

I can see this person's face under the water now, and I see the head gear more clearly. In each one of the 'spines', I think there must be air. I can see the metal hat or helmet has extremely thin tubes extending out by the sides of the eyes right onto the temple. Then there are big clear lenses covering the eyes, which enable the person to see underwater.

There is also a thin tube pressed to the face across the cheek. It looks like a very thin headset microphone, and actually hooks into the side of the mouth, so presumably it supplies the person with oxygen. Another interesting thing is that this person can close down their nostrils without having aid to closing it. There are flaps inside the nose which shut down like a dolphin's blowhole. The flaps close over, so they don't have a problem with getting water up their nose, as long as the mouth is kept closed. So the very fine tube that goes in the corner of the mouth must be an oxygen supply, and if indeed, that is what they breathe. I assume that they can swim wherever they want to? They have very long fingers with extended skin in between the fingers a bit like webbing. They swim very fast with great expertise, and can dive fairly deep. So I think they must have a different type of body to humans, even though it looks similar. Ptplec is telling me that their internal organs are very different to ours; much more compact with a lot less intestinal tract; the body shape is very slender, and the person I am seeing is either not wearing anything, or has some kind of suit that looks like a skin. It looks metallic silvery/green/blue, and not stiff but flexible.I am told the reason that this person is diving into the water is because there is food down there, so I assume the sea is the equivalent of a garden for them. The types of things they might harvest are molluscs, seaweed or fish.

Elaine: I find this extremely interesting! I am now being shown a picture of this 'female human' that I am watching, eating a raw fish, and she has very tiny but extremely sharp, triangular teeth.

Question: Does she have any ears?

Elaine: I can't see any ears, because of the helmet that she has on.

Question: Are there any colours?

Elaine: Do you mean colours on her skin? Her skin is very pale, with a kind of blue green cast to it, almost like you would get on shiny silver, although this is not a very good way to describe it. Imagine if someone was sprayed with silver paint, it's like that but not as intense; so it's silvery, but it has a reflected blue green tinge to it.

Elaine: Now I'm being taken inside the dome, and it's really strange! I see the woman, and she is going in through a kind of an entranceway which opens and closes without her having to do anything. She then leaps into the air onto a semicircular platform which sticks out of the wall of the dome.

There are lots of these platforms, and she jumps up to one and then onto another; and then up using four or five platforms, almost to the top of the dome. Here the dome is open and there is fresh air and sunlight, and she sits up there eating the raw fish that she has just gone down into the sea and caught.

When she has finished, (and bear in mind that she is up at the top of the dome on a platform, at about 10 foot from the top of the opening in the dome), she jumps the huge distance back down into the centre of the dome onto an area which is very soft. She is really very athletic, and she just takes a leap with her arms outstretched, lands on the floor and then walks off. It was just as if she was diving into the water, feet first. It seems as if these people are very fit, they are strong and their bodies are very pliable.

Question: Is the central area in the dome a common area?

Elaine: Yes. When you say a common area, yes, there are lots of people crossing through it, milling around, but not that many that she would hit somebody if she jumped without looking. On the floor of the dome there seems to be lots of semicircular things sticking up from the floor, like the backs of chairs. They are like three quarters of an oval, and it's the same shape as the platforms that are sticking out of the wall that she jumped up on before.

They are semicircular, and there are rows of them around the edges of the dome on the inside. If you didn't know what they were, you would think they were seats with just the seatbacks showing. But as far as I can see there is nothing to sit on.

Now I see her (from the centre where she dropped down), walk down an aisle in between the seatbacks, (if you want to call them that) and out through another door via another quadrant of the dome and back into the sea. She comes back with another fish, and she goes to one of the seatbacks, and she slides something up in the middle, and a hole opens in the floor and she drops the fish in. So, I wonder if it's some kind of a keep net that goes into the water so that she can go fishing and put her fish in there because it's hers. Then maybe she will do something with it afterwards?

I have no idea about that, but I am just watching her putting the fish in, and then slide the thing back down. Now she is going back to the centre of the dome, and on the right-hand side there is a kind of table with someone sitting there. It's in the sunlight because the top part of the dome is open. She puts a piece of metal or plastic like a poker chip or token, with something written on it onto the table. There is somebody there who is keeping a record; she doesn't say anything, just puts the token down, waits for a second for it to be recorded and then puts it back in her pocket.

That's interesting — a pocket. I didn't notice that before, so she must be wearing some kind of a suit, and it's a strange silvery blue-green like her face. It is difficult to tell and you would hardly know if it was her skin or a suit, but it has a pocket in it, so it must be some kind of clothing.

Oh, and now I see alcoves with counters in between the doors on the dome, and people are bringing things for exchange. So, my thought is that if she is catching fish, and then maybe she will take all of her fish and exchange them for something else. Perhaps barter with someone for whatever it is they bring. All I know is that there is some kind of exchange going on.

It feels very much like everything is very closely monitored and is very tight. When she jumped up to the top of the dome and ate the fish, she was looking around and watching to see who was watching her. This was almost like an animal would do if they found a piece of food and did not want to share it with anyone. So it doesn't feel like everything is happy and carefree, it feels more like something that the people have to do to survive; something that is imposed on them, such as how many fish you have caught and that they keep a record of it. It seems they also keep a record of what you exchange it for. What you come in with and what you go out with is written down. Also, how long you are in there is written down too; it's very much a regulated situation.

Elaine: I am asking Ptplec where she lives, and now I see her go out of the dome.I am seeing a kind of a monorail outside the dome that stretches right across the water back to the land. It has long tube-like 'glass' carriages, and she gets into one of those and goes very fast across to the land on the other side of the water. She has with her a bag with something in it; this monorail doesn't just go to the edge of the land, it goes on from there. Everything is very flat until you get to what looks like a mountain range, and the earth is really very red. As far as you can go it is flat, and then wow, up comes this huge wall of red rock for as far as the eye can see in either direction.

She obviously must live there *somewhere*, at least I assume that she does.

Question: Do you get any sense of their method of communication?

Elaine: Well yes, I am being shown that it is 99 per cent telepathy and 1% vocal tones, and I am told that the vocal tones are only used (and this is a quote), for mating or if the person is startled or put in a fear situation. Then, it manifests as a kind of a squeak, very high, like a high-pitched chittering or whittering. I don't know how to describe it really.

Question: This all seems very businesslike. Is there any sense of joy or happiness there?

Elaine: To be truthful, no! This person looks like they've got an 'animal' nature, very suspicious, with eyes down all the time. Her energy is very private, not gregarious, in which everyone would interact joyfully with everyone else; it's as if they are being watched all the time.

I feel like the things that they do are for survival only, and they don't like it very much. It feels as if they don't have the capacity to see a way out to do anything else. It's almost like a prison in a strange way.

When I say that, there is freedom to live, but it seems like the level of intelligence with this woman is limited. I know she enjoyed the light, but when I tuned in to her feelings, it felt like the whole fishing and bartering thing was something that she *had* to do, or was being made to do, because there was no alternative. Another feeling that I get is that she is looking for a way to escape, or to get back to her own habitat.

Question: Does the Andromedan Ptplec have any comments?

Elaine: Yes I'll ask him that, because the person who was sat at the desk in the dome who took her chip to see what she had caught for the day felt as if he was on a different mental level to her. He didn't have to do the fishing, because he was taking the details down.

So I'll ask, what is the point of showing me all of this?

Initially Ptplec tells me that his mother suggested that he show me this imagery as a kind of continuation of the discussion on weather, and it followed on to look at an example of a planet which functions with so much water, which could quite easily happened to our planet at sometime in the future.

Ptplec: As you were enjoying the observation so much, I thought that I would let it continue so that you could get into the feeling behind the inhabitants of this planet although it wasn't my intention. There is no lesson to be learned from understanding or feeling the nature of this woman. It's just another one of the many billions of types of people that there are out there in the Galaxy that are functioning and adapting to the nature of their world.

Elaine: I have just come back to the big mountain range 'wall' and then been shown that this woman can climb really well. But she cannot fly, she can only go so far, but she cannot free herself. I am not sure what sense that makes, but I know that she cannot free herself.

So does that answer the question?

Ptplec now says to me, I can see you have a headache.

Ptplec is going to stop there, and I have a feeling that this session has been influenced by the Sirian who likes to tell stories which illustrate life lessons. There is a possibility I might see something more in it, but nothing as yet, but the visuals were very good.

Chapter 4.

Sensory Telepathic Communication

I have welcomed all the guides as usual, and Ptplec is here straight away. He looks as if he is on some sort of platform and says:

Ptplec: I have been listening to your conversation with Steve about today, concerning this book. I refer to the whole outline, not the contents. I want to go inside your mind.

Note: My friend Steve is the person acting as receiver for this information today.

Elaine: Here I am getting a visual of Ptplec going inside my mind and pulling things out almost like strands of ribbon. I have given him permission to do that if he needs to, and his given reason for this is that he wants to give me the *feeling*, not the thoughts, but the feeling, of the telepathic communication he has been talking about, and the 'being in two places at once'.

I can immediately see a scene which is a view of a planet, and I know instinctively that it is the place where he has his home.

I will just describe it as I see it; I see very white sparkly (what looks like) sand. It's either very fine earth or sand, not quite as white as talcum powder, but like the lightest of sand, and I can see trees that look like palm trees, but they are different to the ones on Earth.

There is a clump of three trees which are bending over, and they have bulges on them, like if you placed 10 rings one on top of the other that became gradually smaller, like Michelin tyres getting smaller as they get to the very top. There are leaves that look like palm leaves, but it's almost like a cartoon representation of what real palm leaves on Earth look like.

It almost looks too solid, like you would see an artist's sketch of an impression of a palm tree. I can see a blue glass, disc shaped house with an igloo style tunnel as the front entrance, built on the sand.

He tells me this is where he lives, this is his home. He is taking me inside now and is demonstrating or allowing me to smell something very fruity and floral, like a cross between how a really strong fruit juice would smell, and the scent of a flower.

Now he's giving me an object like an ornament from a table. It's long and silver, pointed at both ends, and smooth like satinised steel.

Ptplec: The point of showing you this is to demonstrate the power of this kind of telepathic communication which allows you to really be aware of the temperature; to smell the perfumes, experience the touch, and to sense what things feel like as a *whole*. It's not just looking at a picture in your mind this is a whole sensory experience.

Elaine: This feels strange because I can see myself walking around his house looking at everything.

I am now walking around his room, dressed in my pink cardigan and jeans; this is like looking in a mirror! I was going to say it's like watching myself in a movie, but it's not like that, it's much more up close and personal. I also can *feel* myself saying, wow, isn't this all beautiful, isn't the light that comes through this blue glass amazing, it makes everything tinted with a daylight glow.

I almost don't know how to describe the glow, as it's so lovely. It's not harsh, but almost like artists artificial daylight. Outside of the dome, the light is exceedingly bright and it is reflected off the sand too.

I feel as if I would need to squint in order to see properly. I feel that this dome is by a body of water. Maybe it's a sea of some sort and I assume that it would be, because of the palm trees and the sand. I am calling them palm trees, but I'm sure they are not the same as ours on Earth.

Now as a further demonstration of this sensory telepathy, we are now on top of a mountain with snow, and it's cold and very windy. The view is absolutely spectacular; I am so high up that I can see for thousands of miles into the distance. Far away to the horizon, the land looks red and golden. I cannot see much green there, but there is some green down at the bottom of this mountain. It looks like it's very hot down below and far into the distance, but of course on top of this mountain, it's very cold.

And now, in an instant, he is taking me into the interior of a spaceship. The atmosphere, the air, and the feel of it are totally right. Instead of an outdoor feeling — as in smell the fresh air, see the light, — this is a very soft, muffled, well insulated, still place. It has a constant warm temperature to it, and I have gone from somewhere in the ship where the walls were all padded, to a bank of hollow tubes with 'Plexiglas' doors on the fronts. I just *know* that they are sleeping compartments. To use them for sleep, you pull out the half tube, get on, and then slide back in again and close the door. To my mind, this would probably seem less than comfortable, as there is not much space. It would be a bit like being in an MRI scanner!

One advantage though, is that you can see out, because the doors or portholes are clear and quite big. There is a whole block of them, and it would be like being inside of a beehive, where all the compartments or cells in the beehive have a person in each one. Well, it's almost like that except the compartments are round instead of hexagonal, as in a beehive.

Next door to that there is like some kind of galley that has a door you can open and go inside. It's like a 'kitchen', and there are touch pads on the wall, and some kind of fluid or water in there. It is all artificially lit with soft lighting, and lots of material that looks like stainless steel.

Ptplec tells me that it is not stainless steel but something else, even though that's what it looks like. The reason he is taking me to this ship is because he is getting me to feel the surfaces of everything, and to get into the feeling or the sensory information of things like the 'whoosh' noise when the door closes on one of those little sleeping pod things.

The feeling is almost tangible, like a sensation of pressure in my body. This whole atmosphere is hugely sensory. I am able to feel the very still warm air, and this is all part of my experience and learning here.He is demonstrating the beginning steps of where full sensory telepathic communication can take you with visuals; being able to hear, see, smell and touch, and to really be able to feel everything *totally*, so that you feel and know that you are there.

He says that this the beginning stage of being so **'there', that you really are**.

Our internal television, and being a human transmitter and receiver.

Elaine: When I saw myself walking around his house, my energy body or some part of me was really there, and he tells me that the part of me that was there is located in my head, in my brain somewhere. He says it was not my entire energy body, because that is still occupying the space where my physical body is. So I am also very much aware of my physical body here in the room on Earth whilst this is all going on.

So the part of me that went there originates in my head, somewhere in my brain, and it is not a physical bit, but an energetic part from my brain. Maybe it's called my energetic awareness? He is trying to demonstrate to me that if you have your eyes closed and you are not focusing your awareness on the room or the people around you, then you can turn off that outside 'television set' and go inside yourself to the internal viewer. You can get all the same sensations with that internal viewer, like smell, touch, vision, and feeling. The big thing is that this part of you is free to go anywhere. Ptplec says it's the same part of your energy that you use when you go remote viewing, and that it's available to all, as everyone has it located in their brain area.

Question: Is there a way of developing this for everyone?

Ptplec: Yes, for everyone it is the same, and follows on from what I have already been telling you. You have to start to turn off your logical thinking and go into the realms of energy. You Earth people call it so many things, like clairvoyance, insight, and some call it imagination. This is where it begins; you need to cultivate your inner imagination and inner vision. That is why it is so important for people to just sit still, closing your eyes to shut out the external distracting information around you, and focus your attention inwardly.

Elaine: He also demonstrates that there is a point somewhere in the centre of my head where an 'inner television screen' is. He also points to two places behind my ears just above the mastoid bones, and I can see that if I join the three points, this makes a triangle or a triangulation. He reminds me of when his mother (Mir) spoke to me about these two places behind my ears being antenna, or my 'receiving nodes'. He explains that if you were to draw this triangle inside your head, the baseline would be right at the back of your head behind your ears from one side to the other, and the third point would form the triangle at a point in the centre of your head.

Ptplec: It is this energetic triangle that creates the inner vision for you. This triangular antenna enables you to use the inner 'television set', and the 'antenna' and the 'set' work in tandem to locate *where* it is you want to go.

Elaine: I can't say that I understand fully what that means yet, but that is what he is telling me. Now this is interesting!

Ptplec says: You know when you have something wrong with your ears? Humans lose their sense of balance, and sometimes you can also lose your sense of direction. Humans have an inbuilt electro-magnetic sensing device like you see in so many animals, (such as homing pigeons and animals that migrate). They follow electro magnetic pathways which they use for finding their direction. This is an inner directedness, which you can see when whales find their way around the world, for example. Humans have this ability but you are mostly unaware of it and don't use it to a great extent. For example, if you are out in a car somewhere, needing to find a certain place, this guidance system comes into action when you follow your intuition, or you have a 'hunch' that you must take a left or right turn.

So many of you have cut yourselves off from the energy of this area of the brain through fear of being wrong, that you don't use it at all; I encourage you all to change and get used to using it, as it's an important part of the energy that will be much more in use in the future.

Elaine: Ptplec now makes reference to the whole back part of the head; saying that there is so much to learn about energetically-wise in there, and we will be starting to use it to stretch and wake-up over the next coming decade.

Question: Are there (nonphysical) energetic things extending outside the body like these antenna that can be seen in the aura?

Ptplec: No, there are not extended energetic antenna in your aura, but more like energy prints/maps in your auric field. These sort out and contain destination and position to anywhere in the world or Galaxy. For wherever you want to go, it is your homing device, direction finder, or 'satellite navigation' as it were. It's not a one pointed signal which comes out in a straight line, but a whole blueprint or map that has shape and energetic form.

Ptplec: Imagine two little circles at the points just behind your ears, and see that your energy comes out from your body here like a dome or half ball. It's not just a straight line, it is a 180° field and it joins with the energy of the point on the other side of your head to make a 360° field.

This is also part of your sensory guidance system. For example, maybe when you are out, you might feel as if there is someone behind you? Occasionally when out walking you feel someone behind you, looking at, or watching you? When you look around to see who it is, this is when those energy nodes are at work. They give you spatial awareness, directional awareness, magnetic energy awareness; and when combined with your inner television screen, they give you a route map or satellite navigation for when you want to go somewhere mentally, or you need to find a way to physically get somewhere quickly, if in danger. I believe that answers the question?

Elaine: Yes, thank you.

Question: Within the discipline of some martial arts, the highest Masters cultivate high awareness and are able to direct their energy in all directions (360°) at the same time. Are they making use of that same energy field, but translating it into a more physical thing?

Elaine: This is interesting, Ptplec says that yes, they are.

Ptplec: The difference is that they are linking the two points above the ears with another third point above the eyebrows in the centre of the forehead (the third eye point), and that triangulation gives an awareness of your immediate physical surroundings.

Ptplec: When you are tuned in to your 'internal television', it is for you to project yourself *outwards*, and to travel and go somewhere energetically. Whereas the other triangulation point (the third eye) is for detecting what is out 'there' coming in. So for example, if you were trying to sense if someone was going to ambush you; or if you were blind, and trying to be aware of objects in front of you, or perhaps a vehicle coming, that triangulation comes into action and your incoming receiver is at work.

Elaine: So we stretch out our energy fields in one configuration to sense what is incoming, whereas the other triangle to the internal 'TV' is outgoing, for us to travel out on. I find this fascinating!

Ptplec: There are many more incoming and outgoing triangular receiver antenna that link up to different places and other energetic points in the brain. All these different points lock together to form individual triangular antennae. There is one point right on the crown of the head, which is above the 'television screen' area. This is up on the crown where a baby's soft spot (fontanel) would be; and there is also one pointing down, like an upside-down triangle. There are also more than one going down into the energy centres or chakras of the body.

Elaine: I thought he was going to say that there was one into the heart, (which is slightly off to the left of the body), and I think that's connected to the heart energy. But he is saying no, that the energetic equivalent would be more into the centre of the body where the heart chakra is.

Ptplec: This antenna into the heart energy area enables you to be aware of what energy your heart is putting out, and also gives awareness of your physical body, for example, if you have pain or physical discomfort.

Elaine: So, these two points behind and slightly above your ears are *extremely important*, as they are the key anchor antenna points to monitor your awareness of internal and external things. That's amazing!

He's also going on to say how you can use these antenna or sensors to *read* other peoples energy. He explains, for example, that when I am sitting talking to you, I am reading your energy by using you as the third point in the triangle; and that the sad part really was that I didn't know that that was what I was doing.

Ptplec: This is an automatically built in thing for the human body, and it is time to tell you, and for you to know what you are all capable of. This is the time for everyone to realise their potential and to know just how much you will be able to achieve in the future.

You *can* heal and repair yourself.

Elaine: Now he is pointing to a place right behind the bridge of my nose. It's right where my glasses sit on the bridge of my nose. He says, if you go back inside the head maybe two or 2 1/2 inches. It's right there.

He says it is vital that I get this information absolutely correct, and that there is another important point. This is odd; he is telling me that the part I have just been talking about behind the bridge of the nose is like another screen for an internal *camera*. I see a visual of when you are undergoing an operation, when there is a little camera that goes up your nose and down your throat. So at the moment I am now seeing the back of my throat; inside I can see a big artery, and many veins. It's just like one of those television documentaries where you can see what the surgeon sees inside your body.

Ptplec says that *we all have the ability to self direct and self heal*, even when it comes to internal surgery!

Ptplec: The point behind the bridge of the nose (the 'screen') that triangulates with the two points behind the ears is where you can locate, watch, and direct function of internal organs and body systems physically. This is an important point, not energetically but *physically*. This is used if you want to self diagnose or self repair. I know that you have our own physical self repair system, such as when you cut your finger, it will heal by itself. But I am talking about clearing blocked arteries, and everything from strengthening muscles to repairing holes in the heart. This covers anything that the body doesn't generally do without direction or outside intervention.

Elaine: Okay, I accept what you have said, but I can also imagine how a lot of people would say that this is an impossible task or a hard statement to believe. I know they would say that they can't see inside their body, let alone clear blocked arteries! I imagine they would say, what am I doing here—crossing my eyes and looking at the front of my nose? I can also see how it would take lots of practice and people would be resistant to it. Imagine for example, if a doctor came along and said you have got blocked arteries, or an ulcer or something internal that needed to be stitched up, people wouldn't even know where to start, and would be afraid that they might die if they didn't have surgery!

Ptplec: Yes, I understand your concerns, but what I'm showing you is what you will be able to do with practice in the future. I am revealing talents and abilities that you already have; that you use and maybe you didn't realise you used. They are your directional navigation ability, and your intuitive guidance system. I am showing you that there are other parts located in your head and in your energy field that you can utilize to do other things you didn't know you could.

Some people already use these visual aids; I am just showing you where they are located to make it more real, concrete and solid for you, and as I've said before, one day you will be able to walk through walls. That is the simple way of saying that you will be able to change your frequency and pass or travel through something that to a third dimensional person looks like a wall. I am also giving you a part of the blueprint of what all of you will be capable of in the future, because this will start to make it more real and seem more attainable.

It's like saying, well, I've never written a letter before, how do I start? I would say to you—the power to write a letter lies in your hands; and you know that your brain commands your fingers. You have to learn how to write, then once you learn how to write it's something that comes automatically and is a link between the brain and the hands. These things I have talked to you about are the same. They are not familiar to you yet, but if you want them to be, they will.

Elaine: I am going back to the places in the brain, referring to when you were talking about the martial arts, and we came to this point behind the bridge of the nose. I thought about the point underneath the nose, where I believe I've been told that if you hit somebody hard there you can kill them?

Is that correct? I think the premise is that you break the nose and push it up into the brain. I am seeing a visual picture of that and I am feeling that Ptplec is trying to tell me yes, but there is something else that happens when a shock wave goes through that point in the face underneath the nose.

Now something odd is happening; whilst I was trying to understand what he was telling me about that, my perception, my link to him changed. Now my perception is coming via communication from up here at my crown chakra, but going into visual mode here right in front of my eyes. Here I can see the back of my eyes or the back of my eyelids, and right in front of me now I can see his eyes looking directly at me. I saw him blink, and then I've lost the link and what I was looking at. His face materialised right there in front of my inner eyes; I can now see part of his face, about a foot and a half away. Now, my frontal perception of him has gone and I am back up to the crown again, and I don't quite know what is happening.

The feeling I get is that that was a demonstration of the difference between the two points. The usual point is up here (at the front top of my head) on my internal 'television' where I go *out* and see him out there; and then I went the bridge of the nose point to hear and see in front of my eyes, where he was *incoming*. He came in right in front of me, but I still don't know what that has to do with the bottom part of the nose. I perceived that he came and looked at me, rather than me watching him, which is what I have been doing. I was then able to see him looking at me right up close, and it seemed as if it was on the backs of my eyes or maybe it was on my other internal vision screen. There is no other way I can describe it. I am pressing the bit right on my top lip at the bottom of my nose, and it's interesting because that brings my attention straight back to him being in front of me. I don't know whether it's because I'm pressing that part, and that is making my internal vision focus there, or what.

Whereas I saw his eyes and then I lost the internal visual from the crown area, then when I pressed the part under my nose, it brought my attention back to the other 'TV' screen in front of my eyes.

How strange! This is something I think I'll play with and practice to see what I can do with it, because he is not telling me any more, only saying that is enough for today. He says, just play with what I've given you and think about it. Look at your different internal cameras or screens. Think about outgoing and incoming; think about where the energy is situated, and you coming out to see me and me coming in to see you. Because the *me coming to see you place* is very important and needs to be developed and stretched because we will be *coming in* as much as you *go out* in the near future, continuing over the next two decades.

So I don't think that this is just a personal thing for me, it's for everyone. I need to get used to them being right there in front of me, and as a prelude to when I know he is right there in front of me, maybe I can open my eyes and see him physically. I don't know....but I do know that everyone should have a go at this, and test out the points, because we are all going to need them in the very near future, and who wants to be left behind? Not me!!

Now I see him in front of my closed eyes, floating around and turning sideways. I can see I need to find some kind of control over that, and learn how to use it properly. When I touch the bottom of my nose, the change of perception is instant and his eyes are right there, three or four inches away from my face, gradually floating backwards.

Ptplec says, that's enough for today.

Elaine, in answer to a question from Audience: You asked me how my telepathic communication was today, and it was very easy and exceptionally precise. I have experienced that degree of clarity before in many clairvoyant sessions, and I think that it's easy, because that way of working is particular to me. It is one part of me that happens to be well developed because I have used it a lot. I think that some people see visuals in the front (third eye area), probably a lot clearer than I do, because I don't use that area as much any more. I *can* see things there, usually in a television or video screen format, and that tends to be incoming information. Perhaps it's the same place that people see very vivid dreams. Maybe you all remember your dreams, but I don't very often. I obviously have dreams, but I don't remember them in the way people normally do. I think that all of us have all the capacities to do everything that Ptplec has told us about here. However, we've all developed differently and whichever area anyone has used the most is where they find their personal 'doorway' in to see things. If you were a very fit person because you practice sport a lot, you could do things that I can't do, because I haven't trained. Whereas I am good at sewing because I have done it a lot more than perhaps you have. I think the whole range of clairvoyant/telepathic/psychic ability is open to us all. You just have to practice; it's like life. When I first started using my clairvoyant ability I used to see lots and lots of things in my third eye area. Then all of a sudden, one day, I started to see things above my head. It's difficult to explain, but it's as if I have an internal screen which is projected out from the top of my head about six inches away. It felt to me as if I was reaching a deeper level, or a higher vibration of reception. I thought about it, and maybe it's perhaps not higher, just different.

Imagine if you were to put a metal rod through the back of your head, join up those two antennae and turn it 360°! There must be triangulation points *everywhere* in the body for different things! Energy points right the way around the front and to the back, and I bet you every single point has got an amazing function.

Question: Do you think they're related to the chakra functions?

Answer: To be truthful, if it were me answering I would probably say yes, but I couldn't be sure. I don't want to put any kind of preconceived thoughts on that until Ptplec gives me the answer.

Chapter 5.

Clean body, clear mind.

I have welcomed all my guides, and one who radiates light that I call 'The Light Being', comes forward. She says that there is a huge energy force behind you (Steve) at the moment that is pushing you forwards and up towards where you are supposed to be going. It's almost like being on a waterslide, zooming along and bobbing up into the water. It's an upward curve, and in showing me that image, Ptplec has said that he is going to talk a bit about water.

Ptplec: I don't know whether you understand the special qualities of water, or fully appreciate its importance on this planet. Water is not just something to drink or a place that sea creatures live in, it is without question, the total conduit and currency for not just life, but experience as well. As humans, you have no idea how much is contained within a drop of water. You do not realise how much you inhale and absorb the frequencies of water when it falls as rain, collects as fog, mist or snow. In fact, you are absorbing water by breathing when you go outside in any weather at all. Air carries water molecules with it the whole time and information is carried within those water molecules, held and recorded as frequency by the electrical charge. So for example, if you stand by the sea shore and smell the sea air or breeze, you are gathering information on one level (i.e., the smell) about your surroundings.

But if we were to look deeper or close our eyes for a moment and sense further dimensions of what is held in the water, we could gain much more information. This would include the composition of the water, what was happening on the part of the planet the water had come from. When rain clouds blow across from one side of the world to the other, they bring sensory information with them in the form of minute particles of soil and atmosphere from that distant land, and from the seas that they have passed over. Of course you realise that water is being cleaned and energised all the time by electrical energy from thunderstorms which are happening at various times all over the planet. It is also vitally important to consider the vibrational quality of the water which you drink.

Elaine: I am asking him why so important…... As obviously good clean water is healthy for you, I know that.

He is reminding me of how important the influence is, of where water has been. For example, the water from our taps has been through the sewage preparation plant, has been disinfected, chlorinated, and been through all kinds of processes and had fluoride added, etc.

Ptplec: Not only does this type of water contain chemicals, it contains information from the land, the stones and everything it has touched; in truth, the information in one drop of water is much bigger than you realise. So it's good to drink bottled water, and good to drink from springs and natural fountains.

Elaine: The reason he makes such a point about the importance of this is because the human electrical body or 'body electric' needs a certain vibrational quality in the water in order to be in optimum working mode.

He is saying this because he was talking to me last week about energy points in the brain, and especially the two nodes behind the ears; how they connect across the back of the head and form triangulations to various points in both the body and brain.

Ptplec: In order that the triangular connections and the output and input signals are the best they can be, it is vitally important to have access to filtered or pure water for drinking, if you cannot, then obtain the best you can get in any given circumstance. This is because you need optimum working of the triangulation points within your energy body, as you use them to take you beyond where you are now into telepathy, remote viewing, and energy transfer from one place to another. To be able to see inside your body and repair it; to be able to see and know what the quality of energy is like in every chakra point all over the body. So once you have learned to use them, you will see that they are *vitally* important to the *new you* that will develop as time progresses.

When we shift fully into the New Age that people talk about, you are all going to need these skills; how to look inside your body to see if there is anything wrong, how to transport your energy to somewhere else if you wish, and how to speak telepathically to one another.

Elaine: So Ptplec has raised an important point here; the clearer and cleaner your body is, and the less time you have to spend neutralizing unwanted frequency vibrations in the water, the better.

Question from Audience: Is there something that we should be actively doing to water to make it cleaner and purer? Could we perhaps put a spin on it or use magnets or something like that?

Elaine: He immediately says, yes.

Ptplec: When you speak of spinning, the best you can do with treated water fro home consumption is to spin it through any spiral and/or pass it through magnets. Magnets are probably the best; try passing the water through a magnetised sheath or pipe, so that at the very least, it is of a neutral vibration. With neutral water, you can do anything. It's even more beneficial if it is full of life-giving minerals, but if you have to use water that has been treated, then in order to neutralise it and make it as pure as possible, magnets at the best way to do that.

Elaine: He now says 'Oh Joy, to be in this energy'! And it is making me smile,…I think he gets as big a lift and as much happiness as I do when we do these sessions!

Now he wants to tell me about the importance of **Glutamates.**

Before he begins, here is some information I have looked up concerning Glutamates.

Glutamate in our bodies:

'Glutamate is produced in the human body and plays an essential role in metabolism. Almost two kilograms (about four pounds) of naturally occurring glutamate are found in muscles, in the brain, in kidneys, in the liver and in other organs and tissues. In addition, glutamate is found in abundance in mothers' milk, at levels about ten times that found in cows' milk. There are two forms of glutamate.

Glutamate exists in the "bound" form as a part of protein, along with other amino acids. It can also be found in the "free" form in plant and animal tissues. It is free glutamate which plays a role in the palatability and acceptability of foods. Foods which contain high levels of free glutamate, such as cheese and ripe tomatoes, are often chosen for their distinctive and enjoyable flavors.

Glutamate also plays an important role in the body's disposal of excess or waste nitrogen. Glutamate undergoes deamination, an oxidative reaction catalyzed by glutamate dehydrogenase as follows:

Glutamate + water + $NAD^+ \rightarrow$ α-ketoglutarate + NADH + ammonia+ H^+

Ammonia (as ammonium) is then excreted predominantly as urea, synthesized in the liver. Transamination can thus be linked to deamination, effectively allowing nitrogen from the amine groups of amino acids to be removed, via glutamate as an intermediate, and finally excreted from the body in the form of urea'.

Elaine: This is an area I know a little bit about, but not a lot. He is talking about the group of amino acids and derivatives of the Glutamates i.e. Glutamine, Glutathione, and Glutamic Acid and also — Glucosides? (Glucosides are different I know, that's to do with energy).

Here is a definition for Glucosides:

Glucosides definition:

'Any of a number of compounds, typically extracted from plants, that can be hydrolyzed (decompose by reacting with water) into dextrose (energy)'

Ptplec is saying that Glutamates and Glucosides are extremely important for keeping the brain clean and optimally functioning; for clearing the toxic waste from the brain; and equally important for body energy, which I think is where the glucosides come in to give you energy; so a constant combination of high energy and clear thinking gives you a distinct advantage over perhaps how we normally feel on a day to day basis.

Here is a little more information on Glycosides (different again), as it seems important to this section:

'In chemistry, **glycosides** are certain molecules in which a sugar part is bound to some other part. Glycosides play numerous important roles in living organisms. Many plants store important chemicals in the form of inactive glycosides; if these chemicals are needed, the glycosides are brought in contact with water and an enzyme and the sugar part is broken off, making the chemical available for use. Many such plant glycosides are used as medications. In animals (including humans), poisons are often bound to sugar molecules in order to remove them from the body'.

Elaine: Most people have suffered from 'brain fog' at some point in their life. I know that I have days when the ability to think clearly is gone, or I will sometimes get confusion and a 'fuzzy head' usually due to something I have eaten.

I think this information is all correlating around the information he is giving me about the energy template in the brain. He wants to teach me how to be superbly telepathic, and how to be able to free my personal energy and be able to locate somewhere else, as if I was on a Star Trek transporter.

So.....Glutamates and pure water, all right! Bring them on!!!

Elaine: This is odd; Ptplec is now talking about pink things, so I asked him. What do you mean, pink things?

Ptplec: If you were to look inside the brain, the consistency is viscous fluidity, and the natural state colour is pink. Not grey, as so many people think, but pink. The paler pink it is, the better everything runs and functions.

Elaine: I have absolutely no idea how that fits with anything at the moment, but **Ptplec** says that *in order to be able to use the full capacity of the brain and access more areas*, the more you do to progress towards absolutely crystal clear thinking, the better.

So I ask him the question, okay, how do we get really pink brains? How do we get it from what it normally is (which he tells me can be anything from a kind of sludgy red brown to pink), to lightest pink?

He is giving me some advice now.

Ptplec: The least amount of toxic chemicals in the brain from pesticides, herbicides and food additives, (which I already knew about), the least amount of stimulants,....(oh dear, tea and coffee); a maximum amount of quality organic food with minerals and vitamins in, and water is extremely important of course. To be able to activate *some* of the DNA that is not turned on at the moment, it is optimum if you can be in an 'electro-smog' free zone.

Elaine: 'Electro-Smog' is the frequency pollution of the air waves by mobile phones, computers and a million other electrical gadgets, especially those with standby LED lights. He is saying that it is important to be away from the frequencies of mobile phones, high definition televisions and those kinds of things. My comment to him is: Well, that's pretty hard in this day and age, there are television signals and mobile phone signals in the air all the time. So how do we deal with it?

Now he is asking me to remember back to years ago in the late eighties, when some people I knew used to walk around with copper pyramids on their heads as 'protective' gadgets, and I laughed.

Ptplec: In essence those people had the right thoughts and were working on the right lines. But I can see in this time period that it is not really acceptable or convenient to wear that kind of thing openly. (He gets the picture, I'm sure). There is a way to ground the energy that comes out of the air, to earth.

Elaine: He is now showing me a collar, (his mother's collar actually) and in the centre of this there is a tiny copper rod about 2 or 3 inches long, inserted into her collar at the centre of the back of the neck.

Elaine: OK, so I am thinking, how is that useful or applicable to humans without looking ridiculous?

He is showing me all kinds of different things now, like the chains that go on your glasses around the neck, and also something else that goes around the neck, but I'm not getting the whole gist of what he is trying to tell me.

Now I see a piece of copper winding around the arms of my glasses, which is somehow connected up at the back, but to be truthful, I am arguing with him. Well not arguing, but talking to him, saying, well, if you're going to pick up all this electromagnetic energy and you ground it into a copper rod in your collar, isn't it all going to go down your spine? I can't feel that that would be helpful for humans….. and then he showed me a copper bracelet and a copper ring, which many people wear, and he says that as a half measure, you could wear a copper bracelet, but you would need to wash your hands frequently and you would need to discharge the energy. He hasn't really explained this fully, and I think it's because I interfered by interjecting my own thoughts about it not being good for humans—I think he might know better than I do……I shall be quiet next time!

Question: I know that people can have surgery to insert computer chips inside them for identification. So if you use the right kind of copper, is there not some kind of benevolent use for implanting bits of the highest quality metal actually just under the skin? Is that a possibility?

Answer from Ptplec: Yes, there is a possibility, but not with copper.

Elaine: He is talking about an alloy, that maybe would have copper in it but it would be coated with something so that it doesn't leach into your system and give you copper toxicity.

He repeats, yes, there is a possibility to be able to do that kind of thing; but, for example, if we (the Andromedans) use receiver implants, they are mostly organic, so that they blend and live in harmony with the body.

Elaine: The main gist of what he wants me to tell you is, if we on earth changed the use of our frequency bands, i.e. the frequency bands that we put out for the mobile phones to use, and so on, it wouldn't be as disruptive to our own energy fields as it is now. He also reminds me that in our future in the UK they are changing the television band from analogue to digital, and then they will allocate the analogue band to the mobile phones.

He tells me this will be better than it was with regards to being detrimental to our DNA, but it will then affect different parts of the body. He's telling me that we will have to monitor for problems with heart, eyes and liver. Once the mobile phones come down through the spectrum into the analogue range, these are things to be considered.

As our main focus of attention is to the brain, with brain chemistry, DNA, and the electrical body of the brain, he says that changing the frequency output band width can only be an improvement. He also tells me that not so far into the future, from a personal point of view, they will bring forward sound technology. For example, we can insert medications under the skin, like slow release chemicals, so that instead needing to take, for example, HRT pills all the time, (if you have the menopause), you can have medication inserted under your skin.

Ptplec says that as a society we will gradually become accustomed to using that kind of technology, but as we progress into the future even more, it will be realised that you can administer any and all kinds of medication using sound. So the actual application of physical things will not be needed in the future.

Question: I am really interested in the idea of medication by sound, and I'm also really interested in the idea of turning on our unused DNA, and it feels like these two things tie in. I wondered if he has anything to say about that. It feels very pure and exciting, like there's lots of potential possibilities to be released with Sound Energy.

Ptplec: Yes, there is some important information to give you on the use of frequency for reactivating DNA. In fact, it's already happening at this point in time. There is an energetic band containing a specific frequency which has been introduced into the field or atmosphere of your planet, which is altering people's DNA as we speak. This alteration is not an instantaneous thing; it can take from two or three months to two years to take effect on people.

And as we have previously discussed, this introduced frequency is primarily to modify the inclination towards violence and aggression in people on planet earth.

We do this for all of you because you must have acceptance of others as being different to the self. If you can extend the hand of friendship to all instead of the fist of war, you will not continue along this path that you are on, which is polarisation between those who will judge others and fight for pointless causes, and those who will work together for the common good of all.

It is by frequency that we will expand and enhance your DNA patterning over time; it is by frequency that we can adjust capabilities in people, because if the entire DNA contained within yourselves were activated, you could become anything you wish, at any point in time. As one example, the seventh dimensional beings who visit this planet can appear, or take on the form of anything that they wish to be. So if they feel the need to appear as a human, tree, stone, dog or bumblebee, through intention all that is required is to activate the DNA patterns within themselves of such a creature or a thing.

You know from research that you have seen that your DNA as a human is not so far different from that of a chimpanzee, or a fruit fly. All that is required is to flick a few mental switches to alter your patterning energetically, and to change your molecular structure to become anything you want. Now, as I say this, you obviously inhabit a physical body and your physical body would need to be refined tremendously in order to achieve that, which is why you don't have all your DNA frequencies turned on. If this were to happen suddenly you would probably explode! But as you progress, little by little, different aspects of your DNA will be turned on.

Think about this; in simple terms, what you call 'autistic savants' have sections of their DNA 'tuned up' more fully, and other sections tuned down. Due to this, they can have various and diverse abilities; incredible dexterity with numbers, astounding talent with visual interpretation of their surroundings, or phenomenal musical talents, to name a few areas. Now all those talents and abilities are within everyone, but with the autistic savant, their range of general awareness is narrower than 'normal', and they have one area of the brain that captures all their attention. So it is that a particular set of genes has the predominant resonance over the brain, and the other areas of functioning are less active. So to balance the internal and external life skills, cope with the magnitude of their ability, and retain a degree of what you class as 'sanity', some of their social skills are turned off. Any human being can concentrate and display those talents, but if he or she were to have those abilities *and* all the social skills, you would call him a madman, because it would go beyond genius into what you label as insanity. As such, the human form has not yet learned how to command that degree of awareness and greatness of thinking in conjunction with using external skills in the 'outside world', and stay within the boundaries of what you class as normal.

So you can imagine how you could be in the future, once the two aspects are married together. You would then have unlimited potential, plus qualities and talents that you can call upon and use at any given point in time.

And this is one of the most important reasons why you as humans must learn to master your emotions.

You must learn to be non-judgmental; not to judge yourselves, and to not judge others. The first step is to let all of your focus of attention be in the *now*, and to let everything around you be perfect *as it is*. Knowing that you cannot grasp the bigger picture yet and that everything has perfect order allows you to let everything be perfect *as it is*. Because when you think you see a fault or imperfection in anything around you, you are committing an error. It is an error by judgement, because everything is perfect and complete the way it is. When you come to that absolute knowing, you reach a level of peace inside that says there is nothing I need to do, accept express myself and enjoy. For when you tap into the qualities that you all have of perfect art, musicianship or creativity, should you be plagued or beleaguered by inner emotional conflict, doubt of the self, or punishment and judgement of the self, it then becomes madness, and the talent is wasted because the mind and the emotional body cannot handle it.

So, step by step the frequencies unfold, and our first and primary mission is to help to bring humanity into a state of peacefulness, and that comes partly by taking away or changing your previous position as humans towards aggression. And to expand on this, you will discover in the future as you have seen before, that it is possible to create fourth dimensional music and art, using sound vibrations and frequency. Then as you create your holographic pictures and music in the air, it is possible to take the whole experience, be it visual film or music, and make it a complete holographic sensory experience for all to see.

This sensory experience will have all stimulations, not just the physical senses, with smell, taste, touch, and hearing, but also your energetic body will be stimulated to see beyond what is visual and into the larger concept of what is presented to you. The more you clean and lighten your physical body and refine your energy field, the more the brain is cleansed, giving you the ability to see the bigger event. When I say the word 'see', I do not mean just with the eyes, but you will experience, feel and know deep within yourselves a previously invisible, unheard message, using this extension of the five senses you normally use.

You know, I have talked to you previously about the five senses, using these senses, and the energetic points in the head. The whole reasoning behind all of this is to expand the energetic capability of the brain. My mother previously told you about leaving logic behind, and allowing right brain spatial thinking to dominate; eventually not to be in 'right brain left brain mode' where the signals crossover from left to right, but to be in a whole 'united' mode, where the signals go from the front to the back of the head/brain. (See the book Voices from our Galaxy)

This mode will utilize both the receivers and antennae you have in the energetic brain, your inner reception (or inner television screen), inner sight or inner knowing, and inner sensory telepathy which has no words. The whole experience is a 'felt' or feeling experience.

Elaine: The beginnings of this technology are being created now on our planet. We spoke once before about the musical instrument called the Theremin, where magnetic fields are used to operate the musical instrument. This has gone on to be developed into using electronic energy to create music. The principle is, as you move yourself around a room where this equipment is set up, your body reacts with the magnetic field and you create sounds and music. So it is possible to *dance* a sound, and that exercise of dancing a sound is honing your ability to feel the music, and perfecting your ability to create without thinking. It's an energetic and body *feeling* process, and I am sure the autonomic nervous system comes into play then.

Elaine: He is now showing me a picture I saw earlier, of Jupiter. On the two poles of Jupiter it has now been shown and photographed that there are an incredible amount of x-rays present there. He tells to me to go back and look at the detail again and find more information on that, because what you can apply to Jupiter, you can also apply to Earth. Apparently it has not been documented yet, and he wants me to discover what kind of effect that this has on the planet. This is because there is a lot more solar activity happening, and it is affecting our entire solar system in a huge way, creating things we have probably never experienced before, such as fluctuations in health and emotions, technology and weather.

Ptplec: So many things are keyed into your brain function. Energy and chemicals that sleet down on you from outer space which you have never encountered before will activate or shut down capabilities held in your brains, causing a lot of disruption unless you learn how to deal with it. This applies especially to your way of thinking, your creativity, and your ability to function. Before any enormous planetary change, chaotic energy will always come, and you should *'watch this space'* when it comes to the amount of personal chaos you are experiencing now. You will see a tremendous amount happening to all peoples around the earth, and this is one reason why it is of extreme importance to stay emotionally clear and aware in your minds, in order to stay on top of the wave of change and not be drowned by it.

So **clean and clear** should be your byword, and intuitive based thought should be your leader, because no one who wishes to go forward should get caught in the chaos of emotionally driven thinking that can happen as the future unfolds. You will find it easy to surf the wave-tops of these problems, simply because—if you are centered in the now, you will almost go unnoticed and the problems will not be judged as problems. People who are unaware of what is happening to them and retreat into fear will become totally embroiled in their own small view of things and be unable to deal with the situation easily. There will be some, (and I am now looking at politicians) that will finally understand and say, hang on a minute, this is not where I want to be, and they will change.

Do you have a question?

Question: At this point in time, there are a lot of people that are working on themselves in order to be better receivers of this wonderful new energy that is coming in. So the first question is, is it 1% of the population of the planet who are clean and clear enough at the moment, or is it a bigger proportion of the people? Should we be feeling a great urgency? Because from my point of view, if you start getting fearful and saying, oh dear, the energy is coming in, and I'm not going to be ready, I'm not going to make it, that's obviously not going to be good.

Ptplec: The answer to your question is a simple one. It is not going to be a 1% that adapts and 99% that don't… it is going to be graded process, so there will be those who are absolutely ready, clean and clear, who will be in front and ready to come to our ships and interact with us. Then you will find that there are other people who have the awareness and can watch, see and know, but may not be the first to transport their physical selves to other places. It's rather like when a wave breaks on the shore, it is always the edge of the wave which is the thinnest, and as you go back out into the shallows it becomes deeper; i.e. more people, but only the very diehard people who refuse to change will be at the bottom of the deepest part of the water, metaphorically speaking.

And in truth, those people will possibly choose not to be here on earth any more. For example, in the case of a 'mixed bag' of ability in a family; sometimes the energy of the one who is more aware will enfold the others, and sometimes the energy of the children will enfold the parents. It is a case of grading; there are some that will leave and many others that will follow, and in truth, I would say that we are at a point now where 75% of your world population will find this transition not too difficult.

As I mentioned to you before, many of the indigenous people world-wide who are not caught in Western society's ways, and are more in tune with the earth, will find our arrival and the changes that come with it not difficult to take at all. They will be expecting it on some level, because they are not as complex and as deeply rooted in money, power and possessions as Western society, and those people represent a large percentage of the world population.

So you will see that the few who possibly end up at the bottom of the pile as it were, are those who are at the top of government, power and industry, and refuse to let go of their need to dominate. So fear not, because what your heart, energetic will, and your emotional energy puts out is what counts within this scenario. And even if you leave your physical body behind in order to make the transition, you will be amazed that the path between here and there is but a step away.

Anyone who chooses to leave their physical body behind (and there will be a graded scale with that as well), from those who are 'enlightened' and aware and those who are unenlightened and totally unaware; whilst they all may leave their physical bodies behind, there will be the same natural grading by cosmic law as there will be on the physical planet. This will not be anything we choose or control, but more a natural application of the law of attraction and resonance. Each soul will gravitate to where it matches resonance and naturally belongs.

So it does not matter which way anything happens, even if you left your physical body completely, you would still be here if that was your desire. And (to the questioner) I am not in any way suggesting that that is in *your* particular path, because firstly it is not for me to say, and secondly, I have no knowledge of it. So I tell you that there are many options within this transition, and 99% of them are pleasant and uplifting.

Are there any further questions you have to ask?

Question: Yes, but just for clarification really. In a sense, aggression is physical, verbal and attitudinal. With regard to the people who are already able to be cleaner and clearer now, won't their influence be able to help the others just by their presence, or is there another way that they can help?

Ptplec: If you're asking if people can make a difference, my answer is this. In any earth society at this time, there are the people and the government. Within the government are the warlords, the armies and navies and so on. In general, if you asked the people in their hearts if they really want to fight, I feel the answer would be surely be no. People are more likely to desire simple things such as 'I want to go shopping or I want to live my life peacefully and be able to see tomorrow'. They want to have their sons and daughters at home in safety and they want peace and prosperity; and you will also find that amongst government officials.

The truth will arise, and any governments which are not for the good of the people will fall. If you are aware and unafraid, the will of the people will sway governments. Sometimes there are key people in governments who, because of their rigid policies and selfish desires, no longer need to be in power. So if you take out one blocking pin from a whole rank, then the others who desire a more loving and peaceful world will listen more to their hearts and the people. It is true that as more and more new souls are born as fresh thinkers, they will take their place in society and go into places of power in order to change the way things are done. Part of the transition between aggressiveness and peacefulness will also come because of our arrival, but understand that certain things must be in place before this happens, as we do not wish to be feared, attacked or misunderstood. So there are several key elements to do with truth, politics and government which need to manifest into the open and be seen before we interact with you physically.

Question: So the ET's won't make themselves visible on this earth until that situation with governments change?

Ptplec: Many of us are already visible in the sky, but for the moment this phenomenon as you call it tends to be taken as unreal and dismissed by those who control the media. There is a power structure on earth which denies our reality, because that power structure cannot withstand the threat that they think we pose to their ability to be in power. So the voice of your people could speak with actions in order that they no longer have the power that you give them.

Elaine: If we no longer bought newspapers or believed and paid for all that is broadcast by the television we would be in a position to ask for a new way of communication with truth. Ptplec says that our internet communications system gives us a certain degree of this, as the many who speak the truth have a place to be heard.

Ptplec: The truth of who we are and how we are here to help you will be more visible as time progresses.

Question: And those people who control us such as government and media can welcome and embrace you with no fear?

Ptplec: Our purpose and wish is to give you love and assistance, and to assist you all to become peaceful Galactic citizens.

Steve: Mmmm wonderful!

Ptplec: Remember also that the main reason we are here is because not only is your solar system changing, but the whole Galaxy is going through changes, *and it is time*.

We, from where we are, see that you are entering a phase of change from outer Galactic influences that cannot be stopped. So, it is as if you were in the sea and a tsunami came, we are here to give you our assistance to help you to float. We do not stand by and watch whilst other souls in the Galaxy are in difficulties; and this applies to not just your planet, but others as well. So you are not alone in this. We are all passing through the same changes. We are all encountering different elements that are a part of the growth of our universe.

Question: Is a book the best form that Elaine can be working on? Or is there another means that she can serve the purpose of passing this information on in any clear and loving way?

Ptplec: There are two answers to this question: the internet is faster, but doesn't necessarily touch those people who are unaware of her presence. A book you can pick up in a bookshop, an airport or anywhere can do that; the two avenues go together. It should be freely available on the Internet, and then it can reach the whole world, but also in book form, because it then reaches those who are not likely to search for Andromedans or ET's on the Internet, even though there are millions who do because they are thirsty for knowledge of what could be. They are thirsty for grounded, honest information about what may happen in the next 10 to 20 years. That's our gift, and so the two avenues will suffice for the time being. We ask for perhaps a book on a disc or as an e-download. I can assist in pointing Elaine in the right direction to make it so that those who read what will come on the Internet will want to have the book. She is always open to new suggestions, and radio interviews are also good. That may come in the future.

Note from Elaine: BBS radio called me in August for an interview to go out on November 23rd 2007. Perhaps they arranged that? :o)

Chapter 6.

The Ultimate Power of the Heart.

Elaine: Okay….. An interesting small change has happened today in the fact that normally when I see my guides, they appear to me from my left-hand side going into a semicircle around to the back of me on the right. They all have their particular places, but today for some unknown reason, (and this is the first time ever), I began to see them first, over to my right behind Steve. His Guardian Angel Kohelan and guide Terry are here too, which is a different thing as well. So I had to *really* think about the order in which they came because they're all in different positions; and concentrate more fully to hold them all in my vision.

Strange…..I didn't know how much this would disturb me; it just goes to show that flexibility is paramount in all things, and change can come at any time…so adaptation is the key word! Even though this was only a small thing, I know it serves the purpose intended for me.

Now I welcome Ptplec the Andromedan male, son of Mir. When he first gave me his name, it sounded like teplec. So he spelt it for me, in order I get a 'feel' for it. It is PT(U)PLEC— Like teplec, but with a 'pt' in front. It fits together a lot more concisely than that and sounds a bit Egyptian. He says, perhaps you can understand now why we don't always give or volunteer names, because in our language our names are a 'feeling' visual thing, because we use telepathy all the time. So rather than having to have lips, teeth, and tongue getting in the way in order to say them, our names are visual and pictorial.

Ptplec: You were right Elaine, when you thought that I was going to speak to you about the physical heart and the energy of the heart today.

Elaine: He initially starts off by showing me a cartoon picture of a heart shape in the centre of the chest, which I assume would not be the heart muscle itself; it would be where the heart chakra is. Radiating out from this I can see that there are three lines; one that goes straight up through the neck and head and out to the top of the skull, and the other two go out just as if you had your arms raised up in a vee shape. So, it's a bit like an upside-down arrow; three energetic lines of light that come out from the heart chakra.

He is now showing me that these energetic lines radiate out from the body in all directions. They radiate from the front, back and sides of the body, and always come as three strands together. So you won't ever get two lines coming out from the front, it always has to be three. So again, there is one going directly out from the front, one off to the left side and one off to the right side. They are like arrows, and he says, if you could see your energetic self, you would see something that looks a little bit like a hedgehog, with energetic lines radiating out from back, front, and sides.

Question from Elaine: Before we go on to explain anything else, why _three_ lines? This is very interesting- he's giving me a visual like a child's see-saw on its side. I notice two ends and a balancing weight in the middle; it points out from the front of the body, and out to the sides. The middle is at the heart centre and is what makes an impact or is important. I think it's like you would describe the negative and positive ends of anything, with the centre being the most important and pivotal point. But now Ptplec says don't be misguided into thinking that one side of you is negative and the other is positive, that's not how it works; it's an 'altogether' energy, one and the same thing, so that each strand that you radiate out contains the whole, both elements like Yin and Yang together, but undivided.

Ptplec: There is a flow to this energy; not only does it flow out from the body in diagonal and straight lines in front, but the flow also comes into the body though these strands of energy. And when it comes in, when you are receiving energy and using it in a loving joyful way, it comes in from both sides and is extremely focused in the centre point, which is the heart chakra. *All energy comes in triplets*, from all angles, to be generated from, and to be received into, this *most* important point in the body.

As with all things, there is no good and bad, there is no negative/positive in the 'is it good or is it bad' sense, it's all energy, and it is how it is received and *tuned* within the heart centre, which defines the quality of what goes out. So you can take in energy, and you can do what you will with it and then send it out. There is an intrinsic link with the mind; and the mind and your persona has an influence over what is done with the energy. But, believe me when I tell you, that energy collected here in the heart centre that is directed from the mind, by the mind, for positive purpose and with positive intent, (especially when it is very focused) has a laser like quality to it, because you are drawing from everywhere for that. The triplets of energy that come to all places in the body; can enter at any meridian point or into any of the thousands of acupuncture points on the body; and they all end up being received in the heart area.

The last time we spoke I showed you (Elaine) about antennae and triangulation points in the brain and how you can receive, send out and focus with them. However, this is not your main point of strength, as it were. In a way, these systems are interchangeable, but different. There is a system that works in your head and one that works in your body and heart, and they are both different but interchangeable. So, whilst the brain and the triangulation points are for direction finding, telepathy, or directing your energy body out, (and this is a mental undertaking) you can also interchange and channel that energy through the heart, but to change given situations.

For example, say someone was having an argument in front of you and you wanted to calm the situation down, you could do it a lot more effectively, by telepathically sending the intention and the words down through the heart and out like a laser to that particular person. There are quite a few other uses for this generator of energy, which I will tell you about later on. It is mainly the outgoing energy that will affect your surroundings.

Elaine: So he is just reminding me about the song that says, 'If you can't be with the one you love, love the one you're with' and love the place you are in, give it that energy, and watch it transform.He is saying that the physicality of what it is outside of yourself won't necessarily transform in the third dimension,…. but you are colouring what you see and where you are with a filter that passes through the heart, so that you can appreciate things that were not seen before; you can appreciate fourth dimensional things that were not perceived or recognized before. It's the same principle as looking at something you have, and seeing all the negative aspects of it, or looking at that something and seeing the positive aspects of it. He also tells me that you can use this energy point with these triplets of energy *extremely* effectively for healing animals. And he is reminding me of how I have done this in the past by channeling the energy out of my hands. When that happened, I just put my hands on the horse, dog, or cat and allowed the energy to flow through me.

Ptplec: If you also *consciously* use and direct that energy, watch how much faster the healing results will come by using it in that way. If you want to influence any given situation, I will explain what you can do. For example you may walk into a job interview or into any kind of situation you feel really needs this energy of love in a positive way. You mentally visualise or see it coming down inside your body from mind to heart; see your thoughts and intentions interfacing with this powerful laser triplet that you have there in your heart centre, direct it at every single person involved, and just watch the look on their faces, perhaps a look of surprise or a change in their temperament.

You have the power to calm any situation, whether it is with man or animal, if you use the focused intention of the mind with the power of the heart triplet *together*.

There is a huge electrical field in the heart, much bigger than you have measured before, and also vast cellular memory. Everything that is contained within the brain is also contained within the heart. As so much of your body chemistry goes through your heart, such as blood, chemicals and oxygen in a constant motion, your heart becomes aware of things much quicker (up to seven seconds* see HeartMath Institute) than your brain does, because it's the information centre sensor for everything inside and outside the self.

One of the indicators of this is the way your heart beat or rhythm fluctuates during the day, depending on what you're thinking about or what is happening in your environment. The heart can detect things about to happen that are not perceived yet, in the same way that a dog knows when its beloved master is on their way home, and will show that they know.

This is another reason to focus on feeling joyful, and being in joyful appreciation and gratitude. All the things that I see you look at on the Internet these days about gratitude and thankfulness are very positive signs of ways of being, and this is a good way to promote health and wellbeing.

Question: Would it be a good idea for us to self monitor, maybe holding the fingers over the wrist to notice when we and our hearts are being affected? Would that be useful?

Ptplec: Absolutely useful! As a tool it is very basic, and there is technology available that you can wear which will give you your heart rate, perhaps on a watch readout; but if you become accustomed to being in tune with your pulse, then that is a better way, because it's much more organic and personal to gauge how your heart reacts to any given circumstance.

Elaine: He is going on to say something about the goose bump effect that humans have, and he is talking to me about the chemical release in the body which causes all your hair to stand up on end. And he's told me that for you, Steve, it's a learned response, because the first time you *really* heard the truth, it hit you so powerfully, so emotionally, that you had a surge of adrenalin, which is what made your hair stand on end.

And now you have made the association and use it in a very positive way as a physical signal indicating when something is right. Because when it has been detected by the heart as a real truth, it triggers the adrenaline flow which makes the hair on your arms stand on end, and gives you goose bumps.

Ptplec: So, Steve, you have developed for yourself an automatic notification system which tells you when there's a truth being spoken, and indeed all people could do that if they wished. With some people, they get a feeling on the scalp or some other chemical signal is triggered by their heart.

Going back to the question you asked, it is good to be able to monitor your own pulse, and also as a musician, Steve, I understand that you appreciate and know the length of second and so you don't need a watch for you to time your pulse, you can pretty much gauge as to what the speed or rhythm is.

What I have given you with this visual picture of the heart energy is just the gloss on the top; there are many more applications and subtle levels to this, but I'm going to give it to you in stages, until it becomes, stage by stage, familiar and acceptable. When I add another level on the top you will have a platform for it to sit on, and it won't be too much for you.

Elaine: Now I am seeing something like we see on television programmes, where a spaceship suddenly warps to light speed, and goes *whoosh* into a V shape of energy. Well now I can see a human being doing that, and the energy is coming from here in the heart but the triplet arrow of energy is pointing in.

So instead of the energy pointing out, like you would do when your arms are extended, it's the same shape, but the energy is flowing in the other way. I don't know at the moment what that's going to be, he has just given me the visual as an example of what he is going to talk about at a later time.

He is focusing my attention onto my fingertips now, and is saying what your heart knows, every cell in your body knows too. The heart is a multi level construction with cellular memory and information is stored in the cells of the heart muscle. Information is also stored energetically in the brain. The brain uses its physicality to transform energy around it and to record and store it in the cells; there is a multileveled structure to this information storage. There is cellular memory, transient memory, and genetic memory; then there is incoming new memories; and the cells in your skin (which is why he is showing me the fingertips and the body), are energy receivers and exchangers too, so they receive energy in and also put energy out. In much more simple terms, you have an aura around you which is energy radiating out of your body, and when you are standing close to someone else, you exchange energy and information with that person. This energy information may not always get as far as the brain, but is always being acknowledged and exchanged in the heart energy centre.

So when you touch someone with your hand, this is also a method of receiving energy and directing it up through the body and into the heart for storage and acknowledgement. You must understand that every single atom, every single cell in your body is both a receiver and a sender of information. I also make a reference here to what happens when people have a body part removed; the energetic field of the limb or organ is still there, and it will still pass energy and information on to the rest of the body.

Ptplec says that this is a very good example of how it works. Whilst the human form is a container for vast memory and information energy exchange, you then have to take into consideration the next level of how the energy and the information is perceived.

Question: Concerning these triplets of energy coming in and going out. Are the molecules of light more plentiful than the molecules of dark? Are they evenly balanced?

Ptplec: Remember when I said to you everything is just energy; each molecule is like Yin and Yang together, they are both black and white; and what you do with it, or how you send it out or receive it in is up to your personal choice?

Do you favour seeing only the 'black', do you favour choosing the 'white', or do you perceive the whole which is both and neither? You receive energy input into your field as a *whole* thing. If your inner balance of 'dark' is more than your quota of light, that reflects on your whole receiving and sending system. It's the same as how you react to any given statement. For example, take something as simple as the statement, 'It's ok'. Do you see the negative side as in 'This is ok, but not really what I wanted' or the positive, as in 'Everything is perfectly fine'?

For example, when you touch someone you receive information coming in from outside. What you choose to acknowledge from the bulk of the energy and information you get from this person will depend upon your interpretation of it. That interpretation will be coloured by your internal balance of light and dark, Yin and Yang, negative/positive or optimist/ pessimist. That's the only way I can put it. So it's like saying if you saw a walnut in front of you and you were a pessimist, or had an excess of energy focused on the dark, you would look at the walnut and say oh, I will never be able to crack that open, and it will probably be rotten inside anyway, what's the point of having that? Then your energy or what you gain from that perception would reflect the way it was received. The information molecules flowing in would be balanced towards the 'black' and not the 'white'.

Or you could look at the walnut and think, 'What a wonderful thing!' There is a beautiful walnut in there. You don't even consider how difficult it might be to open, or you might even think you'd like to plant it and grow a walnut tree. The energy molecules flowing in would then be white, or light, and there is the difference.

An important thing to remember is that all that information, the good points and the bad points, are there as a whole realm of possibilities within each molecule, and you receive it *all* in. *But what your body filters and brings uppermost is entirely down to an inner choice that gets harder to change the longer it goes on.* You can make a conscious aware choice to change it,(i.e. changing the way you judge and look at things), but it begins when you are young, and is perpetrated by learned responses from others. But in truth, you are receiving all the information, the Yin and Yang about everything and it's just down to you as to what you choose to perceive.

So, if I asked you to you put your hand into a dark hole and tell me what you feel in there, depending on the level of light/dark preference within your cells, there could be great fear, and you could already be anticipating negative things. Or you could be positive and trusting like a child; if you asked a young child put its hand into a dark hole, and the child trusted you, the child would think that it's soft and it's nice and something furry was inside. Whereas, if you're an older person who had a fear of mice, and you felt something soft and furry, you might scream or even be afraid to do it because you've automatically assumed that it is something you don't want to touch, or that might harm you.

I am giving you these simple little examples because I want you to think about it and enlarge, and enlarge again, until you can see that basic bottom line concept, and how it colours everything in the world; how it colours your basic perception of what the world is. And in truth, as with everything, it is multi-dimensional. You can choose to look at one aspect or one dimension of it, choose to look at the whole thing, or even a different dimensional aspect of it. I am sorry to labour the point on this, but it is the foundation for something a lot more profound, which needs to be built on. I need to give you this basis, so you can understand and accept what comes later. So think of yourself as a living breathing sponge; a sponge that takes in the water of information and also gives out 'water' too. But we are of course talking about energy and information all the time. And I can feel Elaine is thinking about when she does a 'reading' from a photograph and how she does it.

Elaine: I'll just explain this…. when I do a reading from a photograph of a person, I know that there is an energy captured in the photograph, and I can either put the photograph between my hands to read the energy, or when I am writing that which I am receiving, I hold the picture out of instinct against my heart. So I am writing and receiving the information directly into my heart without it passing through my hands, and now I can understand how that works! So I wonder if you could also use it to 'self diagnose' as to whether something is good for you, like fruit, vegetables, tea, or anything else, just by holding it against your heart chakra and maybe taking the pulse after a few moments to see how your body reacts. Because you don't necessarily need to know the answer in your mind, as your body knows it within its own innate cellular wisdom, and it will react accordingly.

Ptplec: Yes, it is possible to read information from anything.

Elaine: Now he's giving me a visual of the chair that I am sitting on, and the energy triplets coming out from the bottom of my spine into the seat of that chair to analyse; I'm getting a whole visual of what is inside the chair, and even more than that. I see visual information of the stone floor beneath the chair, and beyond that to the building I am in, and also information about what was on the land before the building was built.

Ptplec is telling me that with a little bit of practice and giving yourself enough time and space to do it, this is how you begin to refine our ability to become acutely aware of our surroundings and the energy that is around you.

It again goes back to this multi-dimensional viewpoint; whether you want to look in the direction of the dense or darker/negative side, or you want to focus on the light within the energy that you 'see'.

I am using the words light and dark, but I don't like that term, because that is not what it is at all. It's just a choice of description between two things.

Ptplec says that the more you use the subtlety of what your body and your energy field can do and know, and the more you learn to use it, the faster you will advance forwards into being able to manipulate your surroundings. This also includes how your life works, and how your body functions.

You will be able to sit quietly with your mind and ask yourself if there are some things that bother you in your life; why do they bother you, and what is the learned emotional response that you are dealing with. You can then direct your energy to change that immediately.

Ptplec: I cannot stress enough how powerful your mind is; your mind, your heart, how powerful *you* are. You know so little of what you are capable of doing and you take things you do for granted and do not see what you <u>are</u> doing every day. You are an organic 'machine' that is unaware of itself; you have not seen yourself, or your true beauty in a mirror. You have not seen the energetic picture of what you are, and if you did, which you will eventually, you would become transformed, and then more able to use what you have more consciously.

At the moment, the parts that you *do* use are set on automatic, and they are on automatic through learned responses like 'Pavlov's dogs'. The sooner you become aware that you *are* 'Pavlov's dogs', such as becoming aware of yourself and what you can do and what you don't do, the quicker you will find total freedom from the illusory nature of what goes on around you. This world is and *incredible* place, which is *not* as you see it now. You look out on the world and you think that it is in difficulty with this and that. But in truth, if you could see the overview, there *are* changes obviously,— but the grand design, the *energy* of the earth is more whole than you think.

So, I am going to build upon that which I have already spoken about in stages, so that you can understand more fully. And also next week I will go into the triplets of energy, and how they link with the triangulation points in the brain.

Elaine to audience: Do you have anything to ask before we finish?

Steve: All this information you are talking about seems to be so big, so enormous, that at the moment, it seems quite tantalizing to me. It seems to make sense to purify and to connect, and I believe that we are only semiconscious or half awake; and all this is waiting for us. I suppose I'm feeling a little bit impatient. We are all doing a certain amount to connect, and there seems to be so much more that we could be doing. Ptplec is talking about these steps, and in some ways I don't want to ask questions that would interrupt his flow so that we receive it profoundly, rather than indulge the part of me that says I want it now! Tell me the secrets I want to know; what I'm not doing that I could be doing. Is there a direct way to find out? But from what I understand, it sounds like it's coming at the appropriate time. So is it true that it is impatient of me to be asking questions now, because I need to get the answers step by step?

Ptplec: Yes, you're free to ask questions whenever you want, but you are right. In a way, it is like making a pie or a cake. I can show you the cake, but if I were telling you about the ingredients as they are on my planet, I would need to explain what they were and how they worked before you would understand how to make the cake. And the important thing is that these words I give you are for everyone. I would like the 'manual for awareness of capability' to be simple, and I know that a lot of this will be edited down. But I need it to be something that you can 'eat' in one sitting, and not something which takes you 10 years to chew.

So, I know that Elaine will distill from what I have said into simpler truth, and use pictorial stories to illustrate, so that people in general can understand how different they really are, as compared to what they see when they look in the mirror. They only see the third dimensional visual, they do not see everything else that they are, and that's what I want people to understand.

So yes, it has to come in stages. I've given you a certain amount, now go away and practice. Go away and see what you can do with the first stage, and then when you are comfortable with that and comfortable with touching someone and maybe thinking about what you are actually receiving when you touch, you will be ready for more. So much information is there for you to receive, but it is arriving unnoticed, uncovered, not understood. All I am trying to do is to help you rewire your pathways, so that instead of doing everything blindly you do the same things with your 'eyes' open. It then goes from being subconscious to conscious, and conscious awareness of who you are is *the* first step to progressed enlightenment or whatever you want to call it.

I am talking about conscious awareness of the self in all its aspects. Not just the aspects you have had given to you by your teachers; such as the *self* of the inner self, I speak of the powerful *outer* self. You are the powerful beings that will meet us in the future, the beings that need to learn how to use telepathy, and how to use your finer senses. I use an Earth saying from Elaine's mind; go out of the pigpen and into the dining room, because you are fine beings of fine energy, fine beauty, fine everything. You just don't know it!

Elaine: I am being told a little bit more about the 'light and dark' now. I will try to explain what I am seeing now, as when I was talking about light and dark before, I had lots of visuals of energy rushing in and out. I couldn't recount all of it at the time, because I couldn't get it all into words fast enough. I was experiencing it, I was in it, it was a bit like a yo-yo really, trying to hear him and see what it was he was showing me, and also to get it right. I feel like what I have presented is a poor man's version of what he was trying to show me but I think as it settles in, I will get a bit more eloquent in describing it.

I need to chew it over for a while, but the whole visual of the 'hedgehog' thing was amazing. There was energy everywhere and I still don't know what the energy beams are for absolutely, or what they do, but I keep feeling like what I am saying here is like describing the difference between a brick and steam. How I am relating it is not subtle at all. My description is like the brick whereas what it actually is, is like steam...... light and vaporous.

Elaine and Audience: Now we're talking about Eckhart Tolle and his book 'The Power of Now', and about being in the moment, in the now.

Comment: When you get into total 'beingness', what is there to say, what is there to do? Actually nothing—which is why I (Elaine) said I could understand the meaning and message of the Course in Miracles, but I didn't think I could live on Earth and still follow the teachings.

So, I think what Ptplec is trying to tell me is that once you recognize your being-ness, (who you really are), then get into your doing-ness 'car', and drive all your *doing* from a place of *being*; you can completely and radically change the way you do *everything*.

Instead of doing everything unconsciously, like going to the fridge and unconsciously eating something or throwing a piece of paper on the floor, *everything* you do really becomes totally conscious.

Everyone has said at some time, oh yes, I am trying to be a conscious being, but to me, there is *understanding* it and really *knowing* it, without thinking. And I think sometimes the *really getting it* comes when you strip it right back to absolute simplicity and say well, what does being a conscious being really mean? Give me an example! If I was supersensitive, how would it help me on the tube in London; how would it help me dig my garden, or all those kind of things? Let's put it into practical use because when we go out into the Universe, we are going to need to put all those fine sensitivities to practical use. That's how the Extra Terrestrial's work. They use what they've got, but you first have to know that you've got it! THIS is what I see he is trying to tell me.

Steve: Yes, and in some ways, what Eckhart Tolle reminded us of is how to just 'Be' in stillness. It seems like the 'doing' part is forgotten or not encouraged, as we usually spend all of our time *doing* things. What Ptplec is teaching us feels like the next stage!

Elaine: Yes, it seems like he has brought us to the still point of now where you *have* to let go of all the rubbish of the past and future. And when you are in that still point, the NOW, then you become *absolutely* aware.

Steve: Yes, you become aware that you are normally a '*doing*' person, but you are also a fantastic *being* person, and that's the brilliant duality, the polarity is great, and that is a wonderful state to be in, and people will celebrate that. Then there is the question of, — where do I go from here?

Elaine: You put the doing and being together. You *do* (action in your daily life) from a place of *being* that is full of fine consciousness and awareness, not unconsciousness. It's like coming up a level of being, because normally we do most things unconsciously. We are on automatic pilot all of the time, and taking all action from a place of being in the now and being totally supersensitive to your surroundings, you will become so much more like a laser; much more effective in everything that you do and create.

Steve: Yes, because when you try to follow a spiritual path and stay centered, when you are in a state of just being, in a sense you can feel like 'why bother with anything'? There's being in the world, being in this physicality, which is quite crude on one level….but once you become aware of doing things or taking action from being-ness, you're not going to fly off the planet…..you're just going to keep this form, but you will be accelerating your vibrations.

Elaine: Yes, and you can start to manipulate your surroundings to create your desired reality, so that your daily world becomes more refined.

The energy you put out when the being and doing is combined is contagious! It feels like we are rehashing a concept that has been known for years and years…. which maybe is true, but suddenly I have a new level of understanding it. Before, it was just words, and now I see the practicality of it, that's the difference.

Steve: Yes, it needed to be understood with words before; it's not as if we have thrown words away. But now there is this experiential feeling of it, and that truth and that feeling is in the heart. That's where it really resonates most profoundly, and it is bringing the heart energy back in, but not getting stuck in sentimentality. It's exciting to think of just receiving and transmitting and really moving up.

Can you see the importance of three? We have the triad, the triplet, everything important coming in threes and it is how you move through dimensions, I guess. I think you're kind of stuck if you've only got two aspects of anything. You bounce in between them, like the two ends of a stick.

Elaine: Yes, three makes it a whole holographic thing. It's like the two are the polar ends of everything, but the three makes it into a working hologram.

Elaine: At this point we started looking at the two shapes, the arrow going out and the arrow coming in.

Steve: So there's the outgoing V and the incoming V. It was when you were talking about the real fast going out into space *whoosh*, and the word that you were using like time warp or warp speed,….. the V is that shape, and the centre of that point is in the heart, with the two energy strands either side.

Elaine: I still don't know quite how that works, but Ptplec will tell me, I know. Over the millennia, a lot of the ET's have lost touch with certain areas of emotion. They have lost touch with what it feels like to experience and know what we know. This is why a lot of them come down and incarnate onto earth as souls into earth bodies, to be in touch with the rawness, passion and the full spectrum of our emotions. It's just that where we are, from the other side of the fence, we are still being controlled by the full spectrum of our emotions. And what we want is to have it all, but not let it control us. For example, as an artist you like having lots of colours on your palette and maybe we have damped down on a lot of our knowledge, like having a limited colour range, and it has become unconscious or subconscious. It's almost like having an ace in your back pocket, and you don't need to get it out and play it until you are well into the game.

There is an inner revelation when you realise you are in the 'now'; when you have everything and *know what it is you have*, and then consciously direct it with *doing*. It's like sitting in a Rolls Royce car but not knowing the power you have. At this moment in time, we are metaphorically driving our life/car with a bag on our heads. But if you took the bag off and with super awareness could see where you were going, you could also see the *power* that you drive with; then you could go anywhere! You wouldn't just be driving around the same old places thinking that this is all there is…you would be out onto the open road, metaphorically speaking.

Steve: For me it's very personal, and metaphorically, it's like the film City of Angels. The ability to be really sensing everything; being alive on a super sensual level and being aware of all those dimensions, through your taste buds, your sense of smell, seeing auras and everything, to me, that's really being alive.

Elaine: Oh absolutely!

Steve: It's awakening to wholeness, and that's experiential. How could you really describe that in words?

Elaine: Yes, it would be really hard…you could only feel it.

Steve: And where it leads to is love, and the way you play and connect with love.

Elaine: We would all progress into a *feeling* world, where words become redundant. Then that would naturally progress into telepathic communication. A feeling is so much more colourful than a word. That's it, that's the bigger picture!

Steve: Then perhaps all you need to do is to learn how to point the way for others.

Elaine: Maybe you are right!

Chapter 7.

The Large Magellanic Cloud

I've just had lunch and it's a lovely day; I'm feeling very relaxed indeed, too relaxed really…. I've just been talking to Steve about how unfocused I feel today. As I tune in now to the Andromedans, I feel like I'm floating around in space. Ptplec has just come in, and he is beaming something at my forehead. I feel it like waves flowing into me, as if trying to sharpen up my edges a bit and make me a bit more focused. I feel very soft, like a soft focus picture, almost too relaxed to receive. Now Ptplec is sending some kind of energy like a laser drill into my third eye area, and he says it is to get me back on track and get my adrenalin flowing a little bit.

I feel clearer now, and I am seeing some really fabulous visuals, along with a telepathic message about the Magellan cloud. I understand that there is a Galaxy in space called something similar to this and I see vast clouds of red and orange dust.

Elaine: here is some information I found later this week from Wikipedia.

'The **Large Magellanic Cloud** (LMC) is a nearby satellite galaxy of our own galaxy, the Milky Way. At a distance of slightly less than 50 kiloparsecs ($\approx$160,000 light –years) the LMC is the third closest galaxy to the Milky Way, with the Sagittarius Dwarf Spheroidal (~ 16 kiloparsecs) and Canis major Dwarf Galaxy (~ 12.9 kiloparsecs) lying closer to the center of the Milky Way. It has a mass equivalent to approximately 10 billion times the mass of our Sun (10^{10} solar masses), making it roughly 1/10 as massive as the Milky Way. The LMC is the fourth largest galaxy in the local group, with the Andromeda Galaxy (M31) and Triangulum Galaxy (M33) also having more mass. While the Large Magellanic Cloud is often considered an irregular type galaxy, (the NASA Extragalactic Database lists the Hubble sequence type as Irr/SB(s)m), the LMC contains a very prominent bar in its center, suggesting that it may have previously been a barred spiral galaxy. The Large Magellanic Cloud's irregular appearance is possibly the result of tidal interactions with both the Milky Way, and the Small Magellanic Cloud (SMC). It is visible as a faint 'cloud' in the night sky of the southern hemisphere, straddling the border between the constellations of Dorado and Mensa'.

Ptplec says that when they (the Andromedans) go out exploring to different places looking at different things in space, in order to take in the entirety of one of these Galaxies or other gaseous nebulas or clouds, they have to observe from a very long way away to see it fully.

Elaine: He says the reason they don't go into the clouds, is because they can't see clearly what it is when they are in it, plus the frequency of the elements within the cloud would interfere a lot with the energetic field around the ship.

Ptplec: We take samples from a distance, by running an energy beam at it, so that we can analyse what is in the cloud by colour spectra or other means. We also collect physical samples, but don't generally go in too deeply as there is the possibility of getting lost. This is because not only are there all kinds of unknowns in there, but also some elements may be unknown to us and could interfere with the organism that is our ship. When the ship is resonating at a more physical level, such as appearing solid inside of an energy field, we are then prone to being affected by outside influences like asteroids or dust, and as you know dust gets into everything!

Elaine: I see something strange now. Imagine the shape of a club on a playing card, but elongated with two loops either side; it looks like an old fashioned hook and eye, and the shape I see is the eye part. Now this shape has turned upside down and is coming closer. So now, when I look straight at it, it looks like a very long nose, with two eyes. Incredible! It is actually someone's face! The long 'nose' that I see reminds me of how an elephants trunk would be, but not detached from the face. It's as if the face has a trunk-like bump from the bridge of the nose to chin. It is part of the face, and not separate; and it stops short at just barely above the chin, and the mouth part is concealed or closed underneath.

I am getting a real close up visual of the right eye, and it has appeared right in front of my left eye. It is almost like a bird's eye, circular in shape with a thin edge to the lid all the way round it. In fact a round bird's eye is a very good way to describe it. So this being or person has definitely different genetic makeup, and it's really interesting to see how their face is formed in the front. I am viewing it so closely it's like looking through a magnifying glass! I can see eyelashes around the eye, not luxurious lashes, just small; I see wrinkles, or wrinkly folded skin around and over the eye, and across the temple.

Well, will you look at that! He is so strange and different! (and pardon me to the being who is kind enough to let me examine him!)

So I ask Ptplec what's the reason I am seeing this?

He says, because you have never seen a person like this before.

Elaine: No I haven't, and I'm getting a close up view so that it will be possible for me to draw him…..

Ptplec is saying that this is going to be one of the illustrations to be put in the book.

Elaine: So this is a different race or species of person,…one I have not seen before, and I am getting minor cross references in my mind to an elephants trunk/nose, and there is a slight resemblance, but not really. This being's face goes flatter on the sides, and back on an angle, but there's some kind of a bulge at the back of the head once you get past the eye. It's almost looks like a round mop cap that you might have worn on your head many years ago, similar to a cook's hat. The back of this being's head goes smooth from the forehead back, but past the eyes, or where our hairline would be, it kind of bulges right out, like a hat shape. The bulge is quite a prominent one; his neck comes up and the shape of the cranium goes right out into a 'shelf' at the back and around the sides.

I have just asked Ptplec what particular talent, if any, this species of people may have, and he is telling me that if we wanted to categorise them in human terms, they would be master mathematicians.

Elaine: So they play with numbers?

Ptplec: They work in binary code, so it is not so much numbers as code. You know how music is laid down on a CD track in binary code? Well that is how they analyse things, and then convert it into binary code.

Elaine: But now he is telling me that there is more than just one level of binary code. Ptplec says there are more than just the patterns of ones and zeros that we understand on earth.

Ptplec: When you look at your binary code, you just see a flat code in front of you, which may scroll up or down or be in blocks. There is actually a third dimensional aspect to binary code.

Elaine: Oh my goodness, I've think I've seen this concept before. For example have you seen the film The Matrix? If so, then you have seen the opening credits of the film where there are green blips are pouring down the screen, and everything is in binary code?

Ptplec: If you lie that imagined screen of blips flat on a surface, there are energy fields that come up from them. We can take any pattern of 2, 4, 6 or 8 etc and draw an energy line up from them.

For example: Take a 4 block of binary numbers, and when drawing lines from each number you would make a pyramid shape by joining the four lines in the middle. Then you would be able to see the energetic 3 dimensional form you would get from that. The complexity will grow if you take six, eight, twelve or sixteen numbers and join them all together in an upright form.

Think about this thing as a whole, because we are now talking about forth dimensional, not binary but trinary mathematics or calculus. In fact the patterns and numbers are not even mathematics because these beings don't use the same numbers as you do on earth. This particular species of people use trinary code patterns/calculus and this way of analysing something, (or putting it into code) to analyse substances like gases, chemicals and the clouds around the Magellan Galaxy I showed you initially.

They use this particular type of coding because it has more dimensions in it than just writing lines of number ones or zeros on a flat piece of paper. This is because all the information about any element, (both energetic and physical) is stored, and there for you to take within the energetic 3D image.

Elaine: Well that's an interesting concept….. I don't know anything about binary code, but I have never thought of it as having another dimension to it.

Ptplec chips into my thoughts now and says,

Ptplec: The code, if you want to call it that, really has many more dimensions to it than I have shown you here, but that's as much as you can understand for now. So with this one chunk of information, I have given you just enough to show you that trinary code has a third dimension, which radiates out above it; and of course, what rises up on one side, must also go down on the other, so the codes have complete geometric form.

Elaine: Oh!...... now this interesting.

Ptplec: This being you have just seen is one of a race of people who helped with the original creation of organic living energy ships. I have talked to you before about how you can create the shape and body of a spaceship around you by thought, in one of our previous communications. I will give you an example of this. If you wanted a particular type of ship to be created, an energetic blueprint is given to you, which you then focus your attention on.

Elaine: I believe that there are ships you can create yourself, but also created ships that you can go and hire or buy (in our terms).

Ptplec: No, never say hire or buy, because we don't use money, and we don't do that sort of thing in our culture. But ships are available, and within them are the central organic living beings, which you would call the 'computer'. This really is the intelligence inside which forms the ship around it and from it. The kind of ships that look solid from the outside, are actually living breathing organic ships, and they are only piloted and directionally controlled by the mind. When you come to build something like that or assist it into being, you have to understand trinary code concepts. When you have a consciousness that can form anything it (or you) desires, you have to give it very specific energetic feelings, along with a multidimensional picture or code of what it is that you want it to create for you.

When you communicate with this consciousness, you give the code or the blueprint for a particular ship. What follows is then a mutual balancing between the two of you. The energy consciousness will give you pretty much the design you desire, but it will adapt it to itself as well, putting its own imprint or 'flavour' on to it.

Imagine saying to this conscious energy, 'I want you to make me a flower, but what type of flower or what colour the flower is, is up to the consciousness. It has the final finishing 'say' as to what it becomes. This includes the fine details on how the ship actually runs.

Elaine: And so these people I saw earlier who have the different looking faces are the ones who create the code? They understand and can read the code, and in our world in our earth terms, must be far beyond our greatest mathematicians.

Ptplec: When they look at, or hold something like a physical element or even a concept of something, they can create with thought. When creating with energy, the direction of the power comes through their fingers directed by the brain, or mind. They can then create an energy pattern or blueprint code which is readable by other conscious beings or energy forms.

You will find this species of being has integrated into many different cultures and on many other planets. They tend to be solitary beings, not given to huge social clans, but they are family orientated. If you explain this in human terms, they quite like small families, but they do not like big crowds. They like to move quickly from their planets of origin and go out into their Solar System and the nearby Galaxies, because they are very highly prized for their skills with mathematics, calculus, and trinary code (there are more codes than this, but for the moment, this will suffice). They use their skill to execute shipbuilding or ship forming, plus many other forms of technology.

Elaine: Ptplec also talks about structures as well, not just intergalactic space ships, but things like platforms, buildings and complexes, such as living, breathing cities. I ask; if these are the architects, or the creators of the design, what about the actual consciousness or the being that they work with as the raw material (can you call it a being because it doesn't have a body?).I ask because I have seen this consciousness before, in a big spaceship, and it was in a huge round cake tin shaped container that was about eight feet deep and about 15 feet across, and when I looked in there, it was like looking into the deep night sky. It was black but with very subtle shades of colour inside and there were tiny bright coloured sparkles of light coming up from the depths. It was busy with 'neuron' activity (if you can call it that). These are such poor words to describe the beauty of what I was seeing. I learned that this being or consciousness creates the whole ship; and that the whole ship was organic, because the being *is* the ship. It was living and breathing and 'being' the ship. It obviously has no physical body, its just energy, but its acutely conscious energy. It can be directed from outside by the beings I described before, and it will direct itself. So I ask Ptplec, who or what are they, and where do they come from?

And now he is making me laugh, kind of pulling my leg, because I can see the opening screen from Star Wars, with the rolling credits at the beginning of the film, (long, long ago, in a galaxy far, far away!) …..and he is taking me to another totally different galaxy somewhere. I know there are trillions of galaxies within a stones throw (metaphorically speaking)….if you look through the Hubble telescope, you can see them….and Ptplec says there is a galaxy out there, which is not that far away in terms of light years (our term) where he says (laughing) It's life, but not as we know it! Hah hah…it's no wonder Mir sent her son….his personality is a lot sparkier than hers is, she is gentler with kindness and the wisdom of ages.

Ptplec: We discovered and visited this Galaxy thousands of years ago, when our ships were obviously not as advanced as they are now, and they were prone to accidents and at the mercy of energy and chemical fields in space and around planets. At that point we had not discovered fully what these fields and energies were; and so we came to the outer edges of this particular Galaxy, and found a peculiarity that engulfed all of it.

Elaine: Imagine how huge that has got to be; when we look at our solar system, compared to a Galaxy, you can imagine the difference in size.

Ptplec: It was told in our history that there was a pearlescent glow that pervaded everything in this Galaxy; it shone like light on a pearl or petrol on the top of water, with many different colours; and this light permeated everything. We found that it was a particular mineral (I suppose you might call it) that gives off this light, when it is near to a Star or it is receiving or reflecting light from somewhere else.

But whether or not the glow is still visible now, it is still there, affecting everything. The people inhabiting the planets and who developed in areas where this cloud was at its thickest, had the long noses (which you saw earlier), which came down level with their chins. The people have the ability to seal the nose down. This has to do with the need to filter the air; and this all pervasive luminescent, pearlescent dust affects people as a stimulant. This cloud of chemical affects certain parts of their brain, and we discovered that too much of it is harmful to them, which is why they need to be able to filter and close down the nose at times when the 'dust' is very thick.

The planets within the solar systems of this Galaxy all had their own atmospheres, but nevertheless this dust penetrates everywhere. Because of this, within this Galaxy, you will find some of the most brilliant minds and the most adept creators anywhere. But they are creators in a physical sense, as far as you can relate to the word physical. But this dust can also be an irritant, and too much of it can send you 'over the edge' as it were. So they have very sophisticated and well advanced breathing systems.

Elaine: As I see the face again, I can describe that the nose is a bump that goes from the chin, continuing right up the face and spreading out at the forehead. I am told that there are chambers in the forehead where the 'air' is filtered before it passes back to the 'hat' shaped area at the back of their heads. I am so excited to draw this, as this is such an interesting being. And now Ptplec is coming back to the rest of the story (we got sidetracked there).

Ptplec: Within this Galaxy, we also discovered what can only be described as a lake or lakes of dark energetic matter that we found was actually many individual creatures joined as one big whole; like as an earth example, frog spawn, which presents itself as a conglomeration of jelly-like substance with many little individual tadpoles in it.

Elaine: This is what I can see now. If you can imagine a big dark lake, (but its not water) it's deep and thick, full of swirling dense energy like black smoke, but its transparent not opaque. You can see into it and it has these little sparkly things inside it.

Ptplec: When we discovered these energetic beings, they were all massed together. We soon found that there were a lot of individuals in there that made up the whole. I will try to put it to you in very simple Earth terms, it was like finding a group of animals, all joined together in one big hive, and then finding that you can take one, and it will be like a puppy! It won't obviously run around after you, but it can be trained, you can talk to it, converse with it, and it will quite readily and happily do what is requested. We found that it could alter its energy field and morph into anything that you thought of, so if you said, here is a mental picture of apple, be an apple, and it would do that!

So progressing into the now, if you feed or mentally impart to it the code patterns for a spaceship, it will mimic that form and realign its molecular structure to form what you desire. So you can see how, when I speak about these things, and I talk about a lake with living things in it, I am talking about a very large group of energetic beings or creatures. These are the only words I can find in Elaine's head to describe it. In Earth terms, the volume of one of these creatures would fill up a house sized space if you opened the roof and poured it in; and if you ask or tell it the right things, it will be what you want it to be.

We discovered that these creatures were without ambition. They were happy to be as they were in the lake, forever and ever the same, reproducing and growing, but had no concept or desire to do anything else. But as soon as we introduced something else to them, they would mimic or mirror and become it; and we found that we could easily remove the binary code or pattern they had taken on, and when asking them to be something else, they would happily comply. So first of all we discovered these lakes of energy beings, and then we found in our travels the very people who could masterfully put these energetic beings to better use than we were doing. We have vast technology, but this was like strawberries and cream coming together, like two things that were made for each other. The mathematicians from that Galaxy became advanced creator beings and when they came together with the willing raw material in the form of these creatures/beings, wondrous things were created! Wondrous things! From this partnership came basic dwellings that were alive and were altogether a totally new experience; living space ships, and a very different way of living for us. Can you see how it radically changed our way of living? It created an incredible shift in the technology that we already had.

Steve: It's such a momentous moment; could Ptplec maybe describe and explain a little bit more? How did the idea of putting these two together come about? Was it one of their races or was it the group consciousness that created this possibility?

Ptplec: Well, in the first instance, when the first of our explorers came across this lake of beings, we had no idea what it was initially, and like all people who make discoveries, we took our time in isolating a part, because we had no idea that it contained lots of separate parts. Initially, it looked like one whole thing. We found it could equally be divided into smaller parts. When you take a scoop of the whole, it will behave like the whole, and we also discovered that there are definitely particular sizes to these creatures. Initially, because it was an unknown quantity, we carefully took it to our settlement for analysis to find out exactly what it was, and how it behaved.

It is told in our history that it was roughly 1000 of your years before these two races (the beings and the energy beings) were brought together. And by that time, we knew what this energy creature could do; we knew how to command it and handle it to a certain degree, but not with the incredible finesse and power that this other race has. We didn't know how far we could take it, until we finally came in touch with people from this race, and introduced them to the energy. Up until then, we had no idea as to how far it could go and we had been using this energy in very small amounts to experiment with.

We found that we could duplicate things, but because they (the energy) were changeable, it was unpredictable. For example, if you take a whole creature, and you visualise and telepathically send an image that this energy being becomes a CD (earth example), that will be fine, it becomes a CD.

You could play the CD, but it is still made from the energy being, and if it is influenced in the right way, it could and would change back at any time. So imagine if you had an Earth car created by this energy, or a vehicle of any sort, and it passed through a field of stronger information, and suddenly it became a stop light or a tree!...Do you understand how dangerous this could be?

I am using your language to describe this, and you now know we didn't have total finesse on how to use this energy being in a grand way. We couldn't quite master how to get it to become something, and then to be able to hold it for any length of time in the form we desired. If you can understand, once it becomes a starship around us, every single person on that ship is going to believe and know this is a starship. There must be no change in that, because if it suddenly became a double-decker bus when we are half way through a time warp, then it would be no good at all! I know you are laughing, as I use your terminology to show you what I mean. To use your language again, we also got to a stage where, because the code was so well developed and the precision so great, we could buy a 'prepackaged' container of this energy with an already programmed code with it. This is loosely on a parallel to you buying a mobile phone and having the Sim card that goes with it.

Steve: Can you return to the question about the moment when these two forces got together?

Ptplec: Yes, we had this energy in our possession for about 1000 years before we became aware that these two entities, the beings and the energy creatures lived in the same Galaxy. Even after we found them, we were unaware as to how good they would be if they were 'married' together.

It took our ancestors as a third party, to bring them together. Having experimented with the energy for a long time they knew what was possible with caution up to a point. When we came in contact with the race of beings from the Galaxy covered in the beautiful pearlescent gas, after a short time we realised the possible potential of putting the two of them together.

Elaine: If these people breathe in the air or gas (covering the Galaxy) with the special chemicals in it, and have an amazing capacity within their brain for code, why didn't they see this energy there and realise exactly what they could do with it?

Ptplec: 6000 years ago, which is only a small amount of time as you measure it, did you know how to make the finest diamonds out of rough pieces of raw rock? Did you know how to build fabulous bridges over great expanses of water? No you didn't, because everybody progresses, and although the raw material was sitting right there in front of you, you didn't know how to make steel, and you didn't know how to grind diamonds. It takes time, and with the right environment for learning and progression you find new ways of doing things and discover things you didn't know!

So there it was, and even though it had always been there, sitting on their back doorstep all the time as it were, it took our intervention to make it happen. Even though we didn't set out to do that, it all came about perfectly. So, we were then able to come together with these people and show them how they could use their phenomenal abilities to a wonderful degree in order to create beautiful things. And of course then, everyone in the universe wondered and wanted to know about what they had to offer. So it is still their custom, when they come of age, to emigrate out from the planet, and travel the Galaxies creating as they go, and being of service. You will find one of these people in almost every community, because they have this amazing ability to take any 'thing' and lock it or convert its energy format into a code, which, when combined with the organic energy being, can create organic living matter as living structures and practically anything you can think of. These people are always most welcome wherever they go out in the Universe.

Do I sense another question?

Steve: Yes, it just must be wonderful to be the race that made this discovery, and then experience the beauty of sharing that with the whole Universe. It must be a fantastic thing.

Ptplec: Yes, well we won't take the credit for all of that because it's a big Universe, and things can be happening anywhere. In fact on the far side of this particular Galaxy unbeknown to us, they did. So other races on their own have also come across this combination as well, but happily now almost everyone knows about created organic matter now.

This energy can be put to many uses, and it has been attempted to use it for destructive purposes by some races. But it's a strange phenomena in the fact that because of its aptitude and ability to change instantaneously without finessed coding, if you turn one of these energy beings into a destructive missile for example, people soon learnt that if they looked at it and thought, that's *not* a missile,--it's an umbrella,… the energy being would change!

Steve: (laughing). The intention of the people!!

Ptplec: Yes, because it's all down to the energy flow and the information that is encoded in the brainwaves, and so you have to learn how to truly harmonize with the energy in order to maximize the benefits.

It is written in our history that we alone made this discovery, but we know now that there were others out there who found it too. It would be like saying that humans are the only ones who discovered fire. But on other planets far away there is also fire, which someone else has also discovered for themselves.

Steve: Can I ask another question? Does that mean that there are similar species and similar lakes of energy beings that can be put together? Or is it this species of being and *this* particular lake of energy that is found throughout the Universe?

Ptplec: Well, we found it most common in this particular Galaxy, and we strongly believe, in fact, we are sure that this particular genetic combination has come into being because of the gaseous cloud which envelops the whole Galaxy. It has to do with particles of chemicals in the cloud, which create or encourage vast intelligence and amazing consciousness which normally would not be there. It's a phenomenon that has been looked at for many years, and we still don't understand all of it.

Imagine how many years or how much time it would take in your time, and how many generations it would take to explore that whole Galaxy; to find every variable and every end result effect of the cloud there. But we do know that one has to be careful. When we go there, we wear breathing apparatus, so that we absorb just a nominal amount of the particles in the cloud. This is because we could not take the atmosphere fully, as it would not be good for our health. It wouldn't cause death, but it would cause aberrations and genetic changes which we don't want, not unless we can control it. So yes, it's a very interesting place to be, because things don't behave in a way that one would assume they ought to. For example, there are trees on some planets in that Galaxy that can get up and 'walk' around and then sit down and plant themselves somewhere else. This adds a whole new dimension to the whole concept of animal, mineral, flora and fauna consciousness and sentience. But our happy discovery was the beginning of an amazing era for many quadrants of our Galaxy.

Elaine: So now Ptplec is saying that this part of the story is complete within itself, because it gives me a new species or race of beings to draw, and also gives me background information on something which is part of their lives. The energetic beings from the original 'dark lake of energy' are used now all through the Andromedan Galaxy. They are used to create ships for space travel. He tells me that he will also go one stage further than that, but that's another story.

Elaine: Okay, so I think he's saying that's a big enough bite of information for now, and that is enough for today.

I just want to say to Ptplec for the record, thanks very much for that. I thought I wasn't going to get anywhere today. I started off by seeing something that looks like a hook and eye, and it turns out to be this being. I just love to see things that way, because I have *absolutely no idea* what it's going to be when I first see it, so I just say what I see, let it emerge, and I eventually get the whole picture. That's when I am totally amazed and I think wow! I could not have made that up if I tried!

So Ptplec, thank you for that.

Elaine: Hang on a minute, there is more!

Ptplec is explaining more to me about these people, and giving me an example of what they can do. Their speciality is encoding but you could also call it analysis. For example, give them a spoon, and they can tell you what the 'code' or blueprint is for the spoon. But they can't do anything with it unless you give them something that will answer or mirror the code, and Ptplec says it is the energetic matter which really is the more flexible of the two. You give it a code, and it will mimic. Like putting an octopus on a red rock and it turns red; it will change colour. I didn't think of this before; he's saying there is a comparison with little elements of what we have on Earth, like animals or marine life that can change colour to match or mimic their surroundings as camouflage. It's a genetic ability; if you could take away physical form from animals or marine life with that ability, so they just become like a cloud of energy (like a soul or spirit), they are then 'form-less'. Then place their energy on or near anything like a chicken, a coloured rock or a coral reef… and they might change to mimic that for protection or camouflage out of instinct. And so in a basic way compared to the beings you described, they take on form, colour and change!

Steve: Ah yes, I see. In some ways I was giving too much credit to the species that do the coding, and somehow diminishing the importance of the energy creatures. Whereas the beings that do the calculus and the mathematics are the directors, with the great brains for analysis, I can't compare that to the natural genetic animal instinct of mimic and camouflage.

Elaine: Yes, isn't it amazing? Show them the pattern and they will be it! I think its fantastic how they can be influenced by a mental intention; one minute it is a spaceship and the next minute a lounge suite!! My mind boggles, and it's almost quite funny!

Steve: And when the two came together, it's like true artistry was born……

Elaine: Ptplec is talking again now, and he says as a race, we can do many things, but it takes real finesse to be able to break down any thing or concept into what we now know is fourth or multi dimensional particle pictures, and to know what the binary and trinary code is of anything.

Elaine: It is so far beyond 'digitizing' anything…… for example like what we can do with music when we burn it onto CD…… but could we do it with making a car from our minds…*and write the car to disc?* ……so if you put it in a machine, it would make a car?

Oh yes…… do you see it? I see the concept, the difference. You would do away with machines, and would bring two consciousnesses together, one with the pattern and other with the ability to mimic, and you get the results.

Elaine: I don't think that it could be used for destructive purposes, because imagine if you were to make it into a bomb or something like that, it would blow itself up when it hit something. That would be stupid, and how could it willingly self destruct? I don't think it would. It might evaporate,… I will have to ask Ptplec for a bit more information on that.

Steve: Well he did say that some races had tried to use it for destructive purposes, but it didn't work.

Elaine: Just thinking beyond all of that, wouldn't it fantastic if we had that ability and the raw materials! I can feel the excitement they must have felt in the moment they discovered it. I bet in the beginning they had to work out how to keep themselves totally focused when in one of the organic 'created' ships. If they encoded it to become a spaceship they wouldn't want anything changing that whilst on a journey! Perhaps that was why Ptplec said that they observe clouds of matter from a distance; perhaps unknown gases or matter would be destructive or disruptive to the organic ship….and perhaps going into the clouds of gas could change the ship because of the strength of the vibrational signal?

Chapter 8.

How our Universe Began.

The Light is always within the Dark

I am going to begin today by saying that I can see lots of different images in my mind of animals. Animals that are not familiar to me, like lizards, snakes, and dolphins, all kinds of creatures, but they are not like the animals that I have seen up till now, on this Earth.

The Andromedan Ptplec is speaking to me and telling me that he planted the seed in my mind of what he's going to talk to me about earlier on yesterday. It has to do with creation and it has to do with 'in the beginning'.

Ptplec: I will tell you as much as we Andromedans know, and our knowledge obviously only goes back so far. I will speak to you of the mystery of where we are, and when I say where, we speak of our Universe. If you could stand back from our Universe, (and our universe is one of many), it would be like a cluster of cells which interface with one another like soap bubbles on the top of water.

So stand back from that, and see that our knowledge encompasses the existence of multiple universes and multiple dimensions within those Universes. But we still have no real truth on what is beyond that. For all we know the bubbles on the surface of the water that I've just described could be in the teacup of a giant somewhere, who lives again in another universe, and so on!

So, I will take you as far as I think I can go. I'm going to take just one Universe, our Universe… with all the Galaxies that are in it. I'll take you to when there was an organisation of molecules, before matter was really formed. We go to a void, which was actually both a void and teeming with energy and molecules of every size, shape composition and frequency as well.

Within the movement of these molecules, sound and vibration is created on two levels; the inner individual signature vibrations of the molecules, and the outer vibrations created by movement. When anything moves, there is sound, and the sound between two small molecules rushing past one another is different to the sound between two larger molecules rushing past one another.

I am going to try to explain in very simple terms that these molecules attracted one another because they give out a frequency, and like attracts like. They attract each other and group together, and from this some of the more basic chemicals that you know of were formed.

I can only compare this to music. When particles collide with one of their own kind, they are sympathetic, they resonate with one another. They are not opposites, but are harmonious with one another, either being the same or a harmonic of the fundamental frequency. They then cluster to form groups and those groups become matter and mass.

Imagine this on a huge scale; first the universe was filled with what seemed like a mist. This was the mist of all energy and molecules rushing past themselves, creating sound; and then as the sound attracted that which was like it, the clusters grew larger, the mist began to solidify into different substances; into dark heavy matter and light vaporous matter, *and the light matter was held within the dark matter.*

So if you imagine the Universe as a ball, on the outer layer was light matter, in the middle of the ball was solidifying dark matter, and in the very centre or the core was the *most brilliant* light matter.

And the light matter from the outer extremities resonated and called to the brilliant light matter at the core; and so it was that the light was calling, by identical resonance, the inner light out of the teeming darkness; and this irresistible attraction created an enormous explosion, which is what you call the 'big bang'. It was an attraction of light through dark into light again, which is a metaphor for life itself. Internally, there is light, externally, we have dark matter and beyond that there is light. So on your physical level, this refers to inner energy or lightness of spirit, then comes the physical denseness of bodily matter, and externally is the soul energy which calls the light from inside you to come 'home'. When this explosion happened in the Universe, or when the light coming through the dark to meet the outer light happened, this is when there was the addition of fire.

Because of this attraction of light to light, the energy moved at unimaginable speed. It moved so fast and the friction was so great, it created intense heat and fire, and so everything ignited. And then the dark matter solidified, and when vision was clearer, there appeared out of the mist and debris, the internal solid universal matter of Galaxies, Nebulae, Stars, and the beginning of Planets. And some of the heavier dark matters like the Central Sun of your Galaxy collected energy around them, and this is how the Galaxies were formed into their beautiful shapes.

Due to this ignition, there was a divergence of elements created by a forcing together of molecules that were not necessarily compatible. They melded together to make things that weren't in existence before, and this is why there is such a large difference in what planets are made of, how they react and resonate, why some are on fire (Suns), and why some are covered in water.

Up until that point when everything exploded and ignited, only things that were compatible were attracted to one another and clustered together. When there was this fierce reaction, like a thermo-nuclear explosion, things were melded that would not have gone together, and new things were created.

So, remember that I am speaking in very simplistic terms, trying to give you a picture of how solid matter and planetary masses came via action into being.

Going on from there, now there was solid matter, some of which was hot, some was cold. And the planets attracted and pulled in compatible molecules, like hydrogen and oxygen, and those that were on fire burned up things around their atmosphere, and without labouring the point too much, this is how your Solar systems and Galaxies were formed.

Now to go on to what happens next……..

Outside of the concentrated heavy-metal/dark matter spheres that are floating everywhere in the Universe, the light still flows. The dark heavy matter became more dense and concentrated, and the light became more expansive. But within that light were still many molecules of gas and chemicals and such, and these were still creating sound. And we are told that there was an organisation of these molecules in the early beginning. This was at the early beginning that we know of, it's not _the_ beginning, but just part of what we think we know.

To explain a little more……..

Attraction in itself _is_ a consciousness; it's like saying; I am a molecule of hydrogen, and I am attracted to you because you're also a molecule of hydrogen; or you are a molecule of oxygen, and in harmony with me. I am attracted to you, so we will bond together in frequency, and form a new molecule which turns out to be water. So, although you may not see and understand that water has a 'thinking' consciousness, on a certain level, consciousness is there.

And when you examine the universe minutely, you will see this consciousness in _everything_. _There is nothing that is without consciousness of some kind._ And we know that there was present, outside of all this, a greater force. This was a greater and more organised consciousness that had the power to direct. It's like music; all these little molecules of consciousness could be likened to random notes of music, and this greater force organised, and knew how to create melody and orchestrate.

And it began to create from within itself, using the raw matter of the universe. It began to create groupings of cells; and we know that the intention behind the greater force consciousness was to animate with energy; to form living creatures.

Now there is something within this I need to explain, and I find it hard to discover the right words to describe it in Elaine's mind. I am talking once again multidimensionally, in reference to the formation of living matter; the physical aspect of an amoeba, a single celled creature or simple lichen that you see on a tree, and also the other dimension of *the energy* that inhabits it.

In every dimensional aspect of anything, the law of frequential attraction is happening. When physical cells or elements come together and form something, (dense matter) they attract the energy in (light matter). For example, the human bodies that you create attract a soul to come in when forming. In order for anything to be complete, energy and matter must meld and come together as one. We will call this organiser of music or creator of organisation, *The Creator*, for the time being, because we don't have another name for it that you would really recognise.

When I was showing you the pictures of the animals, (and there will be more) my purpose was to guide you to the knowledge that absolutely everything has consciousness. Not just animals or human life forms, but even things that you believe are inanimate. In all places in your Galaxy and the Universe, everything lives. *Everything lives!* Rocks live.

I need to show you that what you recognize as consciousness is only one teaspoonful of the whole ocean of what constitutes consciousness. I speak of trees, plants, all things; even the oceans have a consciousness that can be directed.

We will come back to The Creator and the Consciousness; it's like winding up a clockwork toy, setting it in motion, and then letting it walk on its own. These things were Created and allowed to develop, so there is a little bit of the Darwinian Theory in there in the fact that through circumstance animals do adapt and change, but not to the extent that you have previously believed.

We do not all come from the oceans, and the origins of birds are not the same as the origins of elephants. And in truth, what came after the creation of simpler forms, was the world of nature and plants, then the animal kingdom in all its diversity, (if you must call them animals); all came before human form. We don't make a big distinction between plants, animals and man really because everything is created equally; they are all biological life forms, it's just that some things are more technically advanced than others. There was experimentation and re-creation in the animal and insect world long before the form you know as Human was created.

The more that was created and reflected back to The Creator, the more sophisticated the pattern became. And we eventually come to an 'animal' (if you wish this term), which had more ability and power, like vocalised speech. Although when you consider animals on your world, they all vocalize in some way, (even fish) and in a lot of ways they have many advantages over humans, but that's another story.

So I am trying very simply to say that this is how all humankind or people kind began. Remember what I was speaking to you about last week, referring to the beings with the exceptional ability for numbers and calculations; and them having had that ability boosted by the chemical content of the gas enveloping their Galaxy? I can also say that any given circumstance allows different things to develop rapidly in different places.

So, as an example, imagine a whole garden full of flowers. If one flower is given only potash, and another flower has phosphate, they are going to grow and develop in different ways. Circumstance and exposure to different elements dictate rate of development and outcome. Whether it is with people or flowers, you may get different colours and fragrance, different talents and abilities. The frequencies and energies of the surroundings and environment are attracted or repelled by any form, human or plant, and chemical changes occur within the form, eventually altering the genetic code, so that advancement or regression of species occurs.

Change and adaptability is always required in order to survive, as external influences change constantly and everything must change and adapt or eventually end its existence.

Going back to evolving life, we now make a jump to the stage where, when we were evolved enough, we went out into our Galaxy to explore. Here I have to say categorically that many of the creatures that you see on your planet were placed there by other peoples from other places in the Universe, because many of us evolved enough to become interdimensional creators ourselves.

All we need to do is to place light energy somewhere, and the denser matter follows. We can create matter and the energy is attracted and sucked in to it, like a physical body needs and attracts a soul. We can also do it the other way around by bringing energy in, and attracting form to it. First you form the energy, and it separates (like the light inside the dark) into semi solid form with energy inside, and then attracts compatible energy from outside the self. This causes the dense matter to solidify and take whatever form is intended. The cells of matter then take on 'life' and divide and multiply, following the genetic codes within the original energy.

So there are many ways to create. You can do it one way or the other; it is only a preference, depending on what is being created. Well, when I say it is a preference, it does matter, but how many ways can you cook an egg?

So I just need to open your mind to not just the possibilities, but the reality that what you call the law of paradox, where everything is equally true and untrue, it kind of fits with this. Well, true and untrue is not the correct phrase for this. What I am trying to say, is anything that can go forward can also reverse, everything can be done one-way or the other. No, these are still the wrong words.

Yes, if something has a beginning and an end, then it's interchangeable. The end can be the beginning and the beginning can be the end; so everything flows both ways. How you do it is entirely up to the individual. Our intention is the expansion of the human consciousness into understanding a bigger bouquet of knowledge. When we speak of energy flowing freely (he is showing me electricity now, like lightning storms on the earth and electricity grounding to earth), you are on the edge of rediscovering what has already been discovered. I speak of the use of free energy for external use; how to move your awareness into the molecular world and perceive the energy that is passing through you and that which is right next to your skin; and linking your senses to the energy in the fourth or unseen dimension, call it what you will. It is all there for you to harness and use for everything you need.

The whole thrust of where we are taking you even down to the right brain left brain agenda and thinking laterally or thinking one pointedly, (i.e. logic or spatial/lateral thinking) is taking you into this world of energy, where eventually, you become not just creators of physical things like paper and pens and cars, but you become manipulators of conscious living matter, and creators in your own right.

And with this comes huge freedom, and also *great responsibility*. And again this ties in with what we spoke to you about last week; about the energy of the heart, and not creating or doing everything from the mind, which tends to think using only logic. When you want to create something that has physical form and therefore attracts life energy, you create from the heart. This is a different place, a different frequency; the heart is a place of creation.

Elaine: Yes, I understand a little bit better now. What he is saying is that they can only really create using feeling as the primary force, and not thinking.

Ptplec: As with all things, the being we showed you last week, (who has the blueprint and the trinary code in his mind to give to the energy being/creature) cannot 'think' the blueprint code into the creature/being. He needs to feel it; it needs to be pictorial, and multi-dimensional in its completeness.

This can be compared the dryness of writing the word Apple on a piece of paper as compared to imagining a rich juicy apple in your mind, and feeling the enjoyment of taste, smell and flavour, and everything in it from the white flesh inside, to the rosy skin on the outside. That is closer to what I speak about.

Elaine: I am asking him, why does it have to come from the heart? Is this somehow linked in with love? And yes it is, and of course we put a four letter name to this *feeling* that we get.

Ptplec: But this feeling that you get is multidimensional; when you use it, it encompasses everything from 'I love tomatoes' and 'I love a sunset', to the feelings of sorrow, passion, and humility. In reality, it encompasses so much *more*. You take our feelings so superficially.

Elaine: Now I know this may seem crazy, but how could grief and sadness be superficial?

Ptplec: Remember when the ET with a tall head (the long-head) occupied your energy space. When he left your energy field, do you remember how you felt?

Elaine: Yes, I do remember how I felt. I felt like I wanted to laugh out loud, and sob and cry at the same time, but the feeling of ecstasy, joy and everything was indescribable. It was *so* intense in that moment, as I said before… how anyone could live with that feeling all the time and function properly is difficult for me to know as a human. As we are right now, at our degree of development, I don't think it would be possible.

Ptplec is trying to show me the magnitude of how much *more* there is in the way of the feelings that we have now. We are only like the skin on the custard. We can't imagine really how much more there is, how much more intense it *can* feel, and how you could create something in front of you with your feelings, your heart, your power.

We are already learning at this point in time about how much force and creative power thought and intention has.

Just think how much creative power you would have if it came from the heart, which he tells me is many times more powerful than the mind! The mind is a director, an orchestrator, a formulator, and a writer of sentences like; here is a cat; but *heart* gives you the cat with the warmth, purr, the fluff and the personality-everything- *that* is the difference. So even though the mind and heart work in tandem already at times, the extra focus coming through the heart gives you the complete finished item, gives life with dimension.

Elaine: I can feel many questions coming in my mind, such as- How do we do it properly? How do you get there, what's next, and all those kind of things!

Ptplec: Well, come right back to now, because you can only take this one centimeter at a time, as there is no way for you human beings to understand the concept, the feelings, the actuality of it, unless you go step by step through the process. You can't add a column of two's by simply looking at the last number. You have to begin with every single two in the column in order to come to the final sum.

Elaine: So he tells me that step one is to practice as he told us before, by concentrating your mental focus and visualizing from the mind into the heart. Instead of it coming from up here on the head all the time— like when you do spiritual work, meditation, and that kind of exercise, you focus here (the third eye, and above the Crown) where you can visualise and you can see where things come in and out, then send the visual to the heart to send out; and it's fabulous and wonderful. So things come *in* here in the head area, but from there in the heart, you send and receive things in a different way.

Ptplec: In the heart, there is a tunnel shape or a V shape of energy outwards, so you have to practice creating small things, situations or feelings; you have to take your focus from the mind to the heart. It's not like sending love, for example when you say 'I sent love from my heart to yours'. No.

This is about getting *into* the heart energy, being totally focused, and using your heart energy to send the intention.

Elaine: He showing an image of a torch that has a spread beam. He is talking about using your heart, like the ET did in Spielberg's film. You remember, ET had a 'heart light' in the film? I get this visual and feeling that if you could take your head off and put your head down behind your heart in the middle of your body, so that your eyes are looking *through* your heart, and your mind is side by side with the heart; then take all your conscious thoughts and shoot them through the emotional and feeling properties of the heart, so that they become fuller and more rounded. I don't know how else to say it. Steve, are *you* understanding what I am saying?

Steve: I can understand why he is saying that it is not just about trying to use words from the mind. It is both a different concept and a conceptual leap for me; and although I can hear the words, I still don't know how to do it. I haven't got that far.

Elaine: Yes, it is something that takes a tentative try out, and a little bit of practice. It's like remembering to put one foot in front of the other, eventually it becomes automatic.

Ptplec: I am here to ask you to please tell all people to go and try it, because this is where the future is going for you all.

So many of your young people take the substance you call Ecstasy, as they are trying to feel what it is to really *be* in their hearts. They sometimes become addicted to it because of the glimpse it gives them of what it can be like to be expanded in the heart area. But it is nothing like the feeling of the increased vibration of the energy body when you advance in understanding what inner peace and joy really is. And although it may be difficult for parents to understand why children take this route to try and discover new feelings, everything arrives in its right time. Everything is another door opening on the Christmas Advent calendar as it were, because not everyone can be in contact with this level of feeling yet. You each take your different ways towards getting to the right feeling.

We are not saying that you all need to have the knowledge. We are saying that you need to feel the feelings. So some people attempt to go there with chemical stimulants, and with other people it takes a revelation or being in difficult situations. You're *all* trying to get into your heart, because it is inbuilt within your genetic field to do so. This is because you inherently *know* that this is where the answer lies and where the next step is. It's the future.

It is another facet of the war and peace balance; if everyone lived their lives through their heart energy, you wouldn't be fighting amongst yourselves any more; you wouldn't be blowing things up, and you would understand the nature of energy, how to direct it, and how to have all that you desire. So this is why it is so crucial that the things I have to say to you are made available to everyone now. There is no better time than now, because before, the ability to hear and accept it, or even entertain the thought would not have been there.

Steve: Can I ask a question?

Ptplec: Yes please ask a question.

Steve: Are there any people who are already either putting this into practice on earth that we can follow as examples? Are there any who are getting closer to this way of transmitting energy, or living this way of being? I haven't yet got it fully, myself. Is there anywhere I can go, or anyone I can look to, who would inspire me or open the door a little more just buy influence? Because, as I see it, this is all about transmission of energy and frequency; picking things up and generating it in that way, and it would really help me. Maybe there is another way of letting this change of dimension in, by being around something or someone, and by them talking to you or just being in their field and picking up clues?

Ptplec: There is a multilevel answer to your question. Some groups of people have got part of the answer. For example the Buddhists have a piece of that which we are talking about, but it is incomplete; and so have the New Scientologists. They have different piece, but it is incomplete.

Elaine: Yes, I know some film actors and popular singers are into the 'new scientology' stuff, but I have never really read up on it and I don't know anything about it. But I feel also that Steve is asking for an experience, not just words.

Elaine: This is interesting. I am seeing many visual scenarios, and Ptplec is saying that this is how some people really get into the heart energy.

For example, you could volunteer to go and help children who are dying in Africa or anywhere in the world; or you can sit with someone in a hospice who is dying. This is how some people attempt to get into their heart energy, but Ptplec says that it is such a personal thing for each individual; each has their own way. The closest way that I can point to is by telling you to really see beauty, to really see the *absolute miracle* in every grain of sand and every *thing* that there is around you, with gratitude and appreciation.

Take as the example a grain of sand (have you ever seen the incredible beauty and complexity of a grain of sand under a microscope?) To *really* understand this heart feeling, to '*get*' it completely, that every molecule is an absolute miracle of complexity (and look around you, even in your room); to see the *joke of it all,* and feel the simplicity in understanding; to contemplate the unbelievableness of a fibre of wool or a spiders web and the properties it has…. to feel in awe of everything, with pride, humility and joy. The feelings are so difficult to place into words, but if I could say anything to you it would be; open your eyes and see, and then open your eyes, heart and mind again and again to really see and recognise the living miracle in every molecule.

Look at a tree and think about the consciousness of that tree, the genetics of the tree, and the way it conducts its own inner orchestra. Put real thought into that. When a tree or flower knows the Sun is rising, it turns its leaves towards it; it knows the seasons and responds, it has a responsive energy field reaction to human thought and intention. You want more miracles than that? Every single created thing *is* a miracle; and with that kind of appreciation and gratitude and awe, you will start to laugh and cry at how small you are and how *big* you are, compared to a grain of sand.

It seems that these words are too simple and too pat. Just asking you to appreciate everything and see the miracles everywhere in every moment is not enough. It's something I cannot truly explain; I can only point you in the right direction and say; that's the pot you have to dip into, and how deeply you dip, how expanded you become, is up to you.

Ptplec: Elaine has a few things that she tells people sometimes. For example, when you look at another person, bring your eyes back and look at the space halfway between you and them. Start to see the energy flowing around and past them, and the orbs in the sky. Practice this expansion of the senses, and it will be like a child discovering that there is a sweetie cupboard full of new things, just for you. It is both amazing and wonderful; learn, soak it up, be a child, have everything. And from this place comes the energy that I speak of. When I said some people need to go and help dying children, it's because they need to crack their hearts open to get to the softest place. They need to hit themselves with an emotional sledgehammer in order to be humble and thankful and grateful. Some people need to almost die, have terrible diseases or have a near death experience, in order that they come back changed. It is their way to break the armour that they placed around themselves for protection against having to feel all that there is. On your earth life journey, one of the bravest things you can do is to *open your heart* to the vulnerability that really feeling everything brings; to be without fear, and to go forward with courage into change and total openness.

Elaine: I am reminded that this all sounds very easy, and we have all talked about opening our hearts and being vulnerable, but do you *we really understand it* properly?

Ptplec: This is a level of feeling beyond words. This is really going there, it's when you feel the tears that come with it and it's not grief; it's not sadness, its utter blown away amazement and joy. It is a joy beyond anything you have experienced before, it's fully expanded. And then you are on the road to feeling this all powerful sensation; in your terms, and I am using Elaine's words; this feeling is *so* powerful that you would levitate, you would fly. *There* is your next step.—There is your springboard into the pool that takes you free flying.

Through this combination of head and heart and really looking within I can culminate everything I have ever said about taking your five senses, and using the five beyond them. Develop those qualities of extrasensory smell, sight, touch, hearing and taste, and all the things I have been talking to you about as we have gone along, with regards to the energy you hold in your body. These are all layers and steps to bring you towards your jump off of the springboard into free-floating freedom. You may feel like the road to this is covered in stones that block your way, but you will glide past or over them and it will be as if they are non existent, not a problem.

Elaine; I can feel a whole explosion of words and visuals inside my head that he is trying to give to me, but all I seem to be able to do is relate the same principle over and over in different ways.

Ptplec: Until you begin to practice it and really grasp it, and feel it for yourself, you cannot really *know* what it is. Your first step is to just do it.

Elaine: Does that help answer your question, Steve?

Steve: It helps, because I relate to a lot of that; and it also clarifies that once you are in that state, that's all that's necessary. There is not something beyond that as far as we know. And that's good, because it stops you from thinking 'Is this enough'? And those are the things that give me the goose bumps anyway. It's like being in the moment and in the flow. These are the experiential feeling things that do translate into truths. If someone is in that state around you, for example, Eckhart Tolle, (The Power of Now) the influence you feel is wonderful, you don't have to think about it. I understand now that when Eckhart is in that state of being, he is creating his own dimensions where all of this is both natural and possible.

Ptplec: In that expanded state you can reach the absolute joy and fascination of energetic or as you call it, astral travel. It comes as the next step; this is why so many beings in the Universe wanted to go out and take in more; we wanted to find more than what we had. We wanted to find places where we can reflect our energy out, see and experience for ourselves, and also help others to have it. It's like saying, 'look and see what I found! It is a wonderful flower; would you like to see it too'?

It's a thing to be shared, and that is the basis of our desire to go out into the Universe, visiting the many Galaxies.

Steve: That's really beautiful, because any person who gives a gift is not normally on this level. It's the person who receives the gift who says thank you. In this case, being allowed to give the gift and have it take seed and flower is joy upon joy. It feels like that is what Ptplec is talking about.

Elaine: It's like saying I'm already high. I want to go higher.

Ptplec: So now you are seeing part of our creed or our reason to be.

Elaine: I think that will do for the time being, and Ptplec says that he looks forward to seeing us again next week.

Chapter 9.

Up on the Starship.

I have contacted all my guides and asked them to preside over the meeting as usual. I have also requested contact with Ptplec the Andromedan, as my Extra Terrestrial friends were not there immediately when I tuned in. They seem to be coming from far off in the distance. Ptplec has come with his mother, Mir.

Now Ptplec is extending his hand is pulling me forwards. He says, come on, I want you to come up onto the ship today, and as I feel myself going forward a new sensation floods my senses.

How strange! Traveling forwards is like going through water; it feels silky with a slight resistance, and my vision is like peering through still water with a slight ripple on it. Interesting!

I have arrived on the ship, and I will describe it as I am going along. It is all very soft and quiet, all surfaces are 'carpeted' (obviously not carpeted like on Earth), but soft to the feet to walk on. I'm in a curved corridor which bears around slightly to the left; Mir is up in front leading the way, and Ptplec is just a little step in front of me.

The walls of this curved corridor have a kind of silvery sheen to them. There are triangular decorations or markers on the walls; they appear solid to me and they looks like stainless steel. I'm sure they're not stainless steel, but they look as if they could slide back and reveal triangular windows, so that you could look into an internal room or what ever is behind them. I'm not sure that that is what they are, but that's what they look like. The edges of the 'windows' are not sharp and angular; they have soft curves all the way round.

Mir is now beckoning to me, saying 'come', and the implication is for me to stop looking at the windows and come forward.

That's interesting! …. As we go further along the corridor I have a sensation of rushing forward whilst simultaneously walking at a slow pace. It is as if the corridor collapsed like a concertina and took me to the end without my actually having to walk all the steps there. It was like a fast forward in time, it only took a second or two!

And now we are coming to a diamond shaped doorway with (presumed) steel doors that are closed; and she is entering a coded key.

Mir says, 'Just entering the key doesn't open the door'.

Elaine: The patterns on the buttons that she is pressing on the pad look like squiggly lines or sigils, not numbers or anything like that; she says these keys are just to identify that it is her thoughts that are going to open the door. So the process is that she keys in her identity, and then the door opens for her *but with her thought control*. Perhaps this is all part of the spaceship 'knowing her' personal energy pattern?

Elaine: I assume this must be some kind of a restricted area, although I don't think *anything* is restricted here, it just needs to have a closed door for some reason. As I am walking on through the continuing corridor, I now see on the left a larger triangular window. It's wider and longer than the previous 'windows', and with this one you can see through it. I have just looked through the window into the room, and I can see (to put it in the only way I know) 'babies' growing.

It looks like a very futuristic science lab where there are lots of embryos or newly formed babies (I can see they are babies) in a liquid full of bubbles; there are at least three or four Andromedans in the room, working and/or taking care of everything; I don't really know why they're there, but I assume that's what they're doing. They all glance up at me as I look in and walk past, and then get back to what they were doing.

Mir has told me before about how Andromedan babies are formed (see 'Voices From Our Galaxy') but I have never actually seen the place where they all go once they reach a certain stage of their development.

We are walking on past that now, and have come to the very end of the corridor. I couldn't see any more open windows to the sides, but at the end there is a huge uncovered window that looks out into space. The window is shaped like a rugby ball, and as the corridor curves around to the right, the window curves with it. Oh, and now I can see Mir's face is reflected in the 'glass'.

Steve: Could you describe her?

Elaine: Yes, she is very tall, maybe 7 feet at least, her skin is very pale silvery blue; she has the most beautiful eyes, no hair, and she is very slender. She has a very tiny nose with nostrils, and her lips are quite thin. Her head shape has a slightly larger dome to the crown than humans, but not too much. It just looks like their skulls are slightly larger than ours. She has very long arms, not overly long, but longer than humans; very long slender delicate fingers, which move… I don't know, they seem to move slowly, as if they (the Andromedans) are concentrating intensely and taking in lots of information all at once; or perhaps their focus of attention is very 'focused'—that's the only way I can put it!

She actually takes me by the hand now and we have just looked out of the window. I can see many stars out there in the distance, but I have a feeling we are docked somewhere close to a big planet, which is off to the left behind the window where I can't see. There is a definite light glow outside, so I would imagine if the planet we were docked next to was Earth, then we would be about a third of the way to the moon, it's that kind of distance.

As I am looking out at the stars, she takes my hand and is saying, 'come'.

So, we are now going further on around the corner to the right, and oh! I have just seen a different species of person pass by. This person has a much more elongated head than the Andromedans have, and very *very* large eyes; there is a slightly greenish hue to their skin, and the face has very small features. It would almost be like a caricature of Mir; a bigger head, smaller features with bigger eyes, and boney ridges coming from the top of the nose up over where our eyebrows would be, up into a V shape on the forehead.

This person is wearing different clothing. The Andromedans tend to wear silvery all-in-one suits with soft boots; but this person is wearing darker cloth (for the want of a better word). It is a robe with folds in it, it's almost like a coat would be on top of something else. This person looked at me as I walked past, and then walked on. I am going to ask Mir who that was because I have a feeling it was someone important.

Mir is telling me that he would be the equivalent of an ambassador or maybe a representative of an interested race of beings that are 'out there' working in collaboration with the Andromedans on this ship. Mir is now correcting me and saying, (and I think, this being was a she and not a he) that 'she' is just a spokes person. There is apparently a group of them here, and this one comes to the meetings as a spokesperson or representative of the group.

An interesting feature that I've just seen is that this being also has very long fingers with long pointed nails, almost like claws, but not quite. In comparison to earth, it would be like extended nails, such as when a female on earth would file her nails into a point. The E.T's nails curve under her fingers, and I think they are movable, like human nails. So I don't know why my attention was drawn to that, or whether it's even relevant, but I've noticed when you look at the Andromedans hands they don't seem to have fingernails at all. Their fingers are slim and slightly spread out on the ends, almost bulbous but not overly so.

Now I have just seen someone else pass by; this feels like an introduction to the nations! This ET is small, and maybe as tall as a young child of about ten. So I would estimate maybe four feet tall, and has an angular shaped head. Let me see if I can describe this because I just saw it briefly as they passed.

His face (and it's definitely a he) is much more like exaggerated human features. He has got quite high cheekbones and quite a broad face, almost like a square shape; the top of his head appears to be fairly flat, but it comes out at the side to make it very wide up above the temples and around. A good way to describe this is boney, the overhang of the brow comes out quite angular and goes out to the sides of the eyes, and then it softens down around the temples, and this ET has got much rounder eyes, quite deep-set and he has a fairly pushed up nose on the end. And his colour seems to be more like an olive human colour, like a kind of a muddy pale brown if I can put it that way.

I am just wondering, with all these people I am seeing, if there is not some kind of a big meeting going on, or some kind of a gathering.

Steve: Can I ask a question?

Elaine: Yes.

Steve: Do you have a sense of why *you're* there?

Elaine: No, well not really. My initial thoughts were that Mir asked me to come so that I can *feel* these different races, and maybe draw them; but she is actually saying no,… that's not why I am here. So I now ask, then why am I here this week?

Mir: Well, as a representative of Earth, you can listen in to what these people are saying in our meeting.

Elaine: Wow! I am immediately seeing lots and lots of interesting faces here; it's as if I am connected to two places at once. I can see visuals of people in the front of my forehead here, and also up on the top of my crown, above my head.

Mir is showing me a really strange shape; it's in a big auditorium off to the left, which is kidney shaped. The back of the auditorium is semicircular, and the front has circles on both sides and it comes in to a straight stretch in the middle. To my left I see something that is very tall and to describe it, I will have to use Earth terms here. Imagine something that is standing on three legs like a tripod, but extends way up high, maybe 80 feet or taller. From the top of the tripod there are metal pieces spread out like fingers of a cupped hand, and then they are joined in a circle at the top, like an open container. In this container is what I can only describe as an airbag or a balloon, but made of some sort of beige soft material, like silk; and the circular piece is around the circumference of the airbag. It has folds in it and is very soft and subtle, not shiny or smooth, and it's sitting on the top of this tripod thing, supported by struts. Its glowing like a light and it's at the back of the auditorium.

At the front of the auditorium, there is a long bank of seats, with some sort of table in front. It's very nicely curved, like a serpent or a wavy line. There are people sitting there of all different races, and there is a podium in the front, so I think that everyone gets a chance to get up and speak. In the mid-ground there are long rows of comfortable seats like an amphitheatre would be, graduated up towards the back of the room. I am at the back of the auditorium at the moment and I can see the backs of other human beings sitting there.

Steve: You mean other human beings, as from the human race on Earth?

Elaine: Yes, I see them; a couple of them are quite young children, between 10 and 12 years old; and they look very ordinary. On the seats to my right, there are three adults sat in different seats, plus two teenagers to my left, sat about halfway up, and that's it.

Mir is taking me down to the front, and I am sitting in the second row back about three spaces in, so I can see and hear what's going on.

Steve: Can I ask a question? The other human beings there, do you think it's possible that they are in a telepathic state and present in the way that you are? I guess you will be visible to them too; or are they more physically there in body and perhaps living on the ship?

Elaine: No, Mir is telling me immediately in answer to your question, 'are they in a telepathic state like me?', that there are two people in meditation and the others are asleep and dreaming. Then there's me, and I am in telepathic and visual communication. I suppose the part of me that is here is my energy body, like having an out of body experience or being fully projected there telepathically.

Steve: Can I ask another question? Of the other ET's that are there, do you feel that any of them are there in energy only like as in dreams or meditation on the planet or and they in another kind of dimension?

Elaine: What a very interesting question! Are all the ET's really there, or are they physically in some other dimension, and just projecting their energy here?

Mir is now saying, very well observed!

Mir: 40 per cent of them are here physically, and the other 60 per cent are using telepathic bi-location. They are here because they have bi-located in; they look solid enough, but their real physical form is somewhere else. So we see their energetic body, the part which is very conscious, as an energetic representation of them.

Steve: It's fascinating isn't it! Can I ask another question?— So can *you* notice the difference as to whether they are an energetic representation or really there in physical form? Mir obviously knows the difference, but how does she ascertain which is which?

Mir: I can discern by their radiant energy field. The energy fields of those who are really here are much more contained. It is visible, but they keep it at a respectful limit and distance from others. But those who appear as a holographic image or use bi-location to get them here energetically give off a lot more radiant energy, because when we look, we are actually seeing refined solidified energy as opposed denser physical matter. So it's as if they are slightly transparent, but not quite, if you know what I mean.

Elaine: OK. Mir is motioning me to just listen for a moment, and someone has stepped up to the podium to speak. I recognize the speaker as a Sirian being; they are extremely tall, 14 or 15 feet, with a large dome or melon shape to their heads, and this one is dressed as I have seen them dress before, in a beige or cream coloured robe. The sleeves are wide and end halfway down the arm. He has some kind of a book in front of him; it is a blank book, which I am told is there to record everything he says. It's almost like the book is like a big camera lens which records the face of the speaker and the words that are spoken.

He begins by placing his hand on it, and this triggers it to begin recording a record of the event.

Elaine: Right. I'm going to have to really concentrate now and listen carefully to what he is about say.

Okay, this is really interesting stuff! First of all, when I spoke about concentrating on what he was going to say, a very bright light came on in front of my eyes (which are physically closed). Then there was a big whooshing sound and the light flared like a supernova. It felt as if my energy was propelled forward very quickly and as I looked at him

I drew his attention and he looked back at me, acknowledged me and then looked away. And I could see his mouth moving, but I could not hear anything. It was absolute blank silence; and then I realised that I am listening in the wrong way. I have to listen with my inner sight? [like inner sight or inner knowing].... I expected him to talk, but it doesn't work that way.

Its true telepathy! At first I wasn't getting a visual, but after a bit of blankness, it's as if I'm hovering right in front of a huge waterfall of some kind, and I think he is talking about climate change on Earth. He is continuing to 'speak' about water levels rising; not just the things we on Earth have thought about, like the sea rising and coastlines being flooded, but also on an internal land level like rivers becoming much bigger than they were before, and covering land or washing things away.

I think that this speech is heading this way; this is a debate about whether they should interfere, and simply 'pick people up' from Earth who would otherwise be washed away and die if rivers flooded and seas rose suddenly.

For example, if the Amazon River flooded, and the indigenous people were in peril of drowning; this debate is about whether they should pick them up physically and transport them to their starships. The question then arises; and what would we do with them once we got them, and how would we deal with such a large undertaking? He says there is much more to it than just rescuing people. My translation of his telepathic message is very simplistic, and I am also hearing him asking for 'quadrants' of people [as he puts it] to take care of any animal species that could be saved. He points out that when you look at the logistics of that, they could end up with two thousand elephants and two dozen tigers in their care. So he asks the audience, what are you going to do with them all? What? Where are you going to put them? Should they be transported from one place to another on Earth, or taken onto a Starship?

So this is a huge open debate as to how they can address the upcoming problems and difficulties that will change the face of the Earth.

I am also seeing an image of Mars as well, and he is saying that it won't be too long—a matter of 50-100 years--before surface areas of Mars become habitable again! Because the polar caps are melting on Mars, there is going to be an abundance of water and things will start to grow again, things that have been dormant for a long time.

Elaine: Wow, can you imagine that? — Repopulation of other planets in our solar system? My goodness!... that would be amazing wouldn't it?

Elaine: Wow again....I have just seen an ET who looks like she is straight out of the movies!

It's a female, and her face is just amazing. To describe—imagine if you meld a human face with a snake, shape the mouth so it's very tightly sealed and you can hardly see anything there; nostrils like a snake, and the most beautiful eyes, with a very very elongated head at the back?

I was just knocked out with amazement there, because as I looked, I thought, oh…she's got no mouth, and then this snake-like tongue came out, with a split pointed end. It really startled me, and she's got what looks like blue skin, and it changes colour! Goodness me!

Let's see if I can see the rest of the body.

The rest of her looks fairly humanoid in an ET type way, with arms, legs and normal shaped body; but the thing that really blew me away was that it looked as if she had no mouth at all!

Anyway, I am getting distracted here……

Now the Sirian is talking about a time period of about 40 years maximum, when the geographical shape of the continents on our world will be totally changed. He restates within 40 years, and says that's giving a lot of leeway and being very broad with the edges of time here. I think that we can look forward to huge changes on Earth by 2020; he is saying that the next ten years are going to be particularly difficult because of the influence of our Sun. We will experience much more heat, a lot more extremes of weather, and that eventually we will end up with only *one* polar cap which will be reduced in size by about 90 percent. So you can imagine the scale of change for animals and marine life that live in the arctic oceans and land!

I see that they are discussing *who* is going to be taking care of *what*, and asking that whoever volunteers make a binding contract to do so. I think that all the people who are there are pretty much part of the company, so nobody is going to opt out of not doing it, so its just down to deciding who does what.

Mir is explaining to me that there is little or nothing that we can do really, because the Sun will do what the Sun will do. They have a way of measuring what's happening internally inside the Sun, and she is saying that our Sun has just reached a *layer within* that is of a particularly explosive nature and is burning hotter than it has done before. So we can expect many more coronal mass ejections, solar flares and radiation.

Elaine: So the question is …what happens when you have a lot more water and a lot more heat? Everything gets very tropical…and things like insects and mosquitoes grow bigger and multiply more, till we have whole new sets of things to deal with.

I was also just asking her then …what about this frequency band that the other ET's (the long heads) have set up around the planet to calm aggression down?

Mir: Yes, it's in place everywhere now, and the next stage of that is to turn up the intensity. Now that the grid is in place all over the earth, we can pump up the power to broadcast it fully.

Elaine: So I would assume that within the next year, or maximum two years, we should hopefully see huge changes in the way the world conducts itself, with an uprising of people who are on the side of 'no more fighting please! And the words that she is giving me in my head are 'a natural demise of those who resist changes; so translated, I think that it means that the terrorists end up blowing themselves up, because they cant stop fighting amongst themselves, and the peace loving people get together and say, that's enough, we are not having this anymore.

So that would be truly wonderful if that came about! I only hope and trust that she is accurate on the predicted outcome of their frequency intervention.

A new look at energy creatures and Orbs

This is interesting — I have just suddenly thought about the question we raised earlier about orbs.

I know how orbs gather around people who are speaking the truth, or sending out joy and love. If you look carefully at her starship, it's almost like it is one huge orb, or covered by one huge orb. I have seen that orbs have concentric circles within them, and I am seeing that the centre of the orb send out bands, like wavebands……and they are composed of both light and frequency. I can't quite get a handle on what they are…just give me a minute.

Elaine: Well….this will blow you away if nothing else does! [Laughing]

Mir is showing me lots of images, and one of the images is this.

I see an orb on an ordinary plate, looking like a pancake would; I see it folding itself in half, so it's like half a circle. Now I am getting a bit confused, so I asked Mir; I want to know what an orb really is. I tried to clear my mind, and then I got a really clear visual image in my right eye, and I saw an orb from the side view, and it looks just like a jelly fish!!

So I suppose what we must be seeing when they appear on photographs, are the fronts or tops of them? I say this because I saw this kind of long creature; imagine something about two feet long, just like a jellyfish; something that pushes itself through space, with long streams of energy coming out of the cap part. Then there is a kind of internal tail, which I saw wiggling and waving about just like a jelly fish. Mir tells me that they are almost like a species of creature, and they look like a jellyfish does when it swims in the sea.

Mir: Most Orbs 'swim' or fly in the air, and if you could see them in their entirety, instead of just seeing one side of them, that's what you would see. They are attracted to certain vibrations such as joy, truth or excitement, and of course the question has just popped up in my head now; well if some of them look like jellyfish, what happens if you see one sideways, and why aren't we seeing them sideways on?

And ….oh my goodness, she is saying they also have a strong attraction to the light, such as in when you flash a camera. They then turn instantly to face the light, faster than we can think, certainly faster than a jelly fish would move! So when they turn to face the light, what we see on film is the top of the orb 'jellyfish' with the many concentric circles; and she says that in the centre of the thing itself, is the creature, if you want to call it that.

How bizarre! She also says that we are only just at the very beginning of seeing and discovering many more 'energy' creatures, if you want to call them that. There are mostly ones that move so fast you can't see them with your normal eyesight, and she says that there are hundreds of different kinds that inhabit our planet, which we have no idea are there!

She is picking from my mind the information about 'rods' (see the internet for information) as an example. The creatures that we see under the sea swim with grace and ease, and these species swim in the air!

Mir: Sometimes human beings go to the sea to swim. In the sea are jelly fish who want to multiply, and they release all the sperm and eggs and there are then hundreds of tiny jelly fish, looking like tiny miniscule particles floating around. So the creatures in the air are floating around too, sometimes as infinitesimally small particles, and humans ingest them sometimes, as they almost everywhere in the air. They are inside of you sometimes, and they effect you.

Elaine: My question is, in what way?

Mir: Emotionally; sometimes with unexpected changes of emotion. They can affect your body chemistry, some of the very miniscule 'light' creatures can even enter via your eyes, going into the fluid in the eye, and entering into the system that way.

Elaine: Can they hurt us?

Mir: They have been with you as long as you have been here on your planet, and it doesn't seem as if it has affected you in a negative way so far.(smiling)

In general, they move and vibrate so fast that it's as if you are a rock and they will swim round you or don't perceive your physical body, only the energy. But occasionally, the tiny aspects of them, the babies, (for want of a better word), are quietly still in the air, so you can inhale them.

Elaine: This is quite a remarkable theory she is giving me here. There is part of me that says…ppphhhh!!! If I stood up and said that in front of an audience, they would laugh at me. But I can honestly say, I am only relaying what I see and hear from her; and that was a total revelation to me when she turned that particular orb on its side and showed me that it looks just like a jellyfish! I definitely remain open on this one!

Newsflash! Orbs with long 'energy tentacles' have been photographed and reported September 08

As a kind of a parting shot, she says that she wanted us to be very much aware of all new things happening, like suddenly seeing orbs on photographs; and to be absolutely assured that assistance is going to be there for us every step of the way. This applies to both animals and humans, throughout the whole of this period of time when our climate is changing rapidly. I get the feeling that the climate could go the opposite way too, maybe in a couple of hundred years time; or even a hundred years time; and once the level of whatever it is that is beginning to explode and burn now on the sun has burnt out, then we will go back to the planet being a lot cooler, which could mean that the ice caps would form again. Mir says that there is such a lot to teach us about things that live side by side with us in the atmosphere that we do not know about yet.

Elaine: She has now started to show me the bark of a tree, and I get the feeling that there is something that lives or makes its home in the cracks and crevices in a tree, but I can't see what it is. She says that we are going to have to get used to this gradually, because if she gave us too much information too soon, we would either a) want to stop breathing or b) not go outside at all :o).

Mir: Please remember that these creatures have been here throughout the time that you have been here, so nothing untoward is going to happen, even though some people will create 'news' from it and say that it must be a problem, but it really isn't.

Elaine: I have a feeling that the meeting is going on to discuss other things, and so she is taking me back down the corridor now. As we pass by the room with where I saw all the infants, (all the babies that are growing), I have asked her if she will give me more information on that one day; with reference to the chemistry involved, the procedure, and how they do it, and she has said yes, she will.

So that's a new piece of information, that there is definitely going to be growth of life on Mars! I know there is climactic change happening on Mars now, but if the Andromedans or any other races decide to stimulate the growth of trees or plants or grass, then that would be phenomenal....and our Earth scientists would say...Life on Mars yea!!!!

That would keep us busy...wouldn't it?

To the Audience: Have you any further questions?

No.

Just before I finish the link with them, Mir is showing me some other kind of little thing that looks like an insect. You know what a dragon fly looks like? Well this looks like a dragonfly, but its wings are fan shaped.....like ice-cream cone fans, and there's five or six layers of wings, one on top of the other, spreading out like a hand of cards. The wings are striped; the body of the 'insect' has the wings spreading out below the mid way line of the body and the dragonfly 'tail' comes down in a curve, like a drop down L shape, and my goodness it is traveling incredibly fast! The wings are humming and it's like a blur, and now she has frozen it in time so I can see it.

It's amazing! Supersonic creatures, going so fast that you can't see them!

Steve: There is a mass of information here, it's very particular.... and some really good explanations like the one about orbs.

Elaine: Yes! That blew me away for a start! You could laugh almost, it's so strange....

Steve: Especially as they're attracted to light; they must have a reaction to the flash of the camera.

Elaine: Yes, I suppose so, and that must be why you always see the top side of them. Unless of course the 'jellyfish tendrils' are of such fine energy, that we can't see them.

Steve: The information on climate change and possible life on Mars is amazing.

Elaine: Yes, I could definitely see lots of green stuff growing really rapidly; you know, like when desert blooms after one or two days of rain. It's like a big whammy, and you have total change!

Well, it felt to me as if that's what it's going to be like, and they are saying 'just watch this space' because the Sun is just revving up to go into burning a whole new layer of matter, and so I presume it will be and is now burning hotter than before. So wouldn't it be amazing if Mars suddenly started to go green and it was no longer the red planet? Certain peoples of the world (who I won't name) would be packing their bags and getting ready to go and say, 'this is mine' and create biospheres and create general mayhem wouldn't they? :o)

I doubt very much if our ET friends would allow THAT to happen... unless we come with peace and love in our hearts and go with the purpose of sharing.

What do *you* think?

Chapter 10.

Creatures that Mimic

Further explanations of light and dark matter.

Once again I have welcomed all my guides into the room and Ptplec has come forward. I can see he is sitting very casually on some kind of platform above the floor. I ask him what are we going to talk about today and he says, what would you like to talk about?

Elaine: Well, I don't know….

Ptplec: Then let's talk about rhinestones and diamonds.

Elaine: I just have no clue as to what on earth that could mean, but I know that he will explain as we go along, as this must be a metaphor for something. He is asking me to look closely at what I can see in front of me, which is a necklace with rhinestones in it.

He is explaining that whilst rhinestones look like diamonds from a distance, if you really pay attention to them and look closely, even though they sparkle in the same way, there is no comparison really. They don't have the fire and brilliance that diamonds have.

He says that this is a little bit like life; where you can look at something that seems familiar to you, and sometimes jump to conclusions about what it is. But when you look at it more closely, you can see that it is actually something that *masquerades* as something else; or something that is a shadow of something else. But now he is a correcting me and saying no, rhinestones have their value as rhinestones, because they are unique creation, they are just different in their qualities from diamonds.

Oh, and now he is bringing the subject around to something mimicking something else. This links in with what we were talking about previously in reference to the energy creature which will mimic anything you give to it by way of a holographic image or code.

Perhaps that's the point he's trying to make? I see now that what he is trying to convey is about the importance of the 'whole of the thing'.

Whereas rhinestones sparkle, give off light, and appear to be like diamonds, they don't have the same atomic weight, density or strength. Therefore, they don't have the same frequency or quality inside, which is why he's telling me that it is extremely important when you're asking and communicating with the creature/being that mimics, that you have the whole 'picture'. You can't just visualise something that sparkles and looks pretty in a necklace. If you want diamonds then you have to know the precise density, strength and purity in order to reproduce one absolutely perfectly. He is stressing the point that this is a very holistic thing, and that there is not one detail that you can leave out when you are programming or asking these beings to mimic something. If you didn't give the whole multi-dimensional code, you would have malfunctions and weaknesses and all kinds of unwanted things happening.

Steve: Can I ask a question?

Elaine: Yes, go ahead.

Steve: I don't know whether this is what he is trying to say, but I would like clarity please. When you put your attention on something for your own self growth, you ask for the highest option because that is the way you want to go, and you want to resonate at that higher frequency, like mimicking or changing. Is he making a parallel in that area?

For example, is it like when you aren't sure you deserve something, so you say 'I'll settle for this, rather than what I really want'; or should you always ask for the very best and highest you can attain, whether you think you can have it or not…..is there some personal parallel in what he is saying?

Elaine: Yes. One comment that he is making is that the *details* in anything are very important.

Ptplec: The details in every personal case are extremely important, because when given a choice humans will allow their emotional insecurities to interfere, and therefore you will make choices that are not really your choices to begin with. They are compromises.

It's like saying that you would really love to drive a Rolls-Royce car, but think that maybe it's a bit ostentatious or that you don't 'deserve it'. So you settle for a smaller car instead, when in reality what would give you the most joy and make you feel good would be to drive a Rolls-Royce.

And we find it's *curious* that you humans do that; that you feel there are some things you *can* have and some things you don't *allow* yourself to have, for reasons known only unto yourselves!

But yes, it is very important for you to visualise precisely what you want when you plan your future. In your upcoming time, it is vital for you to be very very clear on all the details concerning how you want it; do not leave any areas uncovered. For example I know Elaine was thinking that she would love a house of her own; and she always thinks, 'I *want* a house of my own, but I would like it to come to me with grace. I don't want anyone to have to die and leave a house to me, in order that I have it. I would like it to come to me in the best possible way.

So you cover all the details including how it will come, with grace, with good fortune, and with maximum joy to everyone, and it is this way when you create anything.

When you create using *the mind through the heart*, which we have discussed before, by thinking, planning and considering exactly how you feel about your wishes and your wants, remember to remove limits. Remove all *self imposed* limits, because there are no limits except that which you pull out from inside your fears. Design whatever you want to please yourself in every aspect, as we design our ships for our joy and pleasure. Believe me, having what you *really* want is far easier to accomplish than if you dilute the energy by worrying about whether you really deserve it, can afford it or *should* have it. Leaving 'woolly edges' or negating your hearts desire allows extraneous patterns in that will influence the whole creation and it will not manifest as you want it to.

Elaine: Ptplec is going on to another subject now and he's giving me an image of the sun; I can see it quite closely, a big fiery mass of burning energy. I had to really concentrate and focus with this as he is saying some important things:

Ptplec: In simple terms, your Sun is a big fiery mass of gas, chemicals, liquid materials, metal and many other things beside.

What do you think happens when the last of the combustible atoms or chemicals within it have fused, and there is no more reactive energy; i.e. nothing will burn or explode any more?

The dark heavy matter begins to solidify and you end up with a cooling, solidifying ball of metal, rock, and matter.

Elaine: He is taking me into the middle core of the Sun, and saying that this is a mirror image of Earth in its infancy, when it was cooling, and before any other things began to happen.

I'm seeing all kinds of visual imagery in my mind.

If you can imagine: elements clinging together.....he's talking to me about things still being molten inside the Earth, like a soft boiled egg would be. Soft on the inside and harder on the outside, and he's referring to the 'lighter' matter that also gets trapped inside the centre.

He is saying *'remember that always within the centre of any dark there is always the brilliant or lightest light'.*

I am seeing a vast amount of crystals and things that reflect light, and some are lighter and purer like diamonds and resonate with pure tones (oh I see,… he has come back to diamonds and rhinestones).

Okay, I understand that crystals will resonate, giving off frequency and pulsing energy, and will also *store* energy and information, (as with those that we use for clocks, watches and computers).

Ptplec: I will put this very simply. In the core of something like a planet, initially there will always be a pool of 'light' as atoms or chemicals.

Elaine: I wish I had a better definition of what he means by light and dark! I will have to ask him to explain it to me in chemical terms. Perhaps it has to do with frequency? I don't know…… but there is obviously a clear difference between a quartz crystal and a lump of lead or iron, and maybe the important bit is the capacity to reflect light?

For example, no light, not even x-rays pass through lead. No light gets through or into it, but with quartz crystal, light comes in and sends out rainbow colours, so maybe that's the difference?

Ptplec: Whilst this pool of chemicals is forming into crystal as a central ball shape, you will find that it will be hollow, right in the centre. It continues to be in liquid form all the way through to the surface, and gradually it solidifies.

You will continue to get pockets of hot materials such as you see on Earth, as in volcanoes, where lava still erupts from out of the depths on to the surface of the planet, and as you know, this is how other land masses are formed on the surface of Earth.

Elaine: He is talking to me about the absolute infancy of any planet, and is saying that this is what will happen to our Sun eventually; that it will be transformed into another planet.

Ptplec: Many of your scientists speak about this future event, and say that if the Sun 'goes out' this would be the death of your solar system. I want you to bear in mind that your solar system is moving along with your Galaxy continuously. In the time it takes for your Sun to finish burning and exploding, coming to a state where it becomes a planet, it will be many billions of years into the future. At that point, we will all be in a different quadrant of the Universe, and there will be other Suns that we can take energy from. Besides that, you will also have advanced so far that if it becomes too cold on your planet, you will easily be able to go somewhere else, if you wanted to; closer to another Sun, or to a planet orbiting a nearby Sun. I come back now to the subject of 'the light within the dark' and the centre of any given planet.

The centre of any planet pulses and 'sings' and it's the light, the crystal, the core of the planet that resonates and gives out the frequency from the inside.

Elaine: So I understand that all Planets and Suns send out a unique pulse exactly like a quartz crystal does, which is why we have them in our watches. They fire piezoelectric pulses on a regular beat, and have a constant frequency. Everything gives out a tone, which then becomes the signature tone for that particular planet.

Ptplec says some time ago on our planet, doctors and scientists discovered that if you passed a sound or a frequency through someone's leg or arm muscle, and measured what frequency goes in and what comes out, and discovered the frequency of the muscle inside the leg.

Ptplec: The frequency that emanates out from any planet is determined by its size. The type of crystal or quartz inside sends out a vibration. The comparative size of the centre core correlates with the size of the planet, and therefore it is the union of the two which gives the planet it signature sound.

And so it is for every sphere in your solar system, and indeed the Galaxy. So each one has its own particular tone, and this tone affects all living beings and all living things on the surface of the planet and gives them a 'type'. Because of the particular resonance of the earth, the type of species on it is human.

Elaine: If this is so, what about all the animals and plants?

Ptplec: I am not referring to shape; I am referring to genetic makeup and living systems, type of tissue, one such is what you call 'meat'.

Do you understand that kind of thing, such as systems with red blood cells? Believe me when I say that there are many many other types of bodily systems found throughout the Galaxy. Some of which you would probably have a very difficult time in understanding how they could possibly work. For example, you are carbon based beings, whereas many of the inhabitants of other places are silicon based or nitrogen based.

Elaine: Part of my own thoughts come in here and says 'Pardon? Nitrogen based? How can that be? But I am just going to listen to what he is saying, and not ask questions right now. I am seeing different shapes and sizes of beings, arms and legs and things like that; and he says there is no end to the diversity of species within this Universe even down to (as we spoke about briefly before) living plants that can move on their own.

Ptplec: I am so glad that you cross referenced with your colleague two weeks ago about the trees which can take up their roots, walk to somewhere else and then replant themselves, because these are all sentient creatures (if you want to call them that). Just because their 'flesh' is of a slightly different cellular make up to a human, they still take in air, they still pump plasma around their bodies and they have a consciousness. For example, trees and plants know what they like, such as water and sunshine, and they also sense and know when there is danger, fire or chemicals and they behave accordingly. So, just because they do not make 'vocal' noises, does not mean to say they do not have innate intelligence.

So there's a point that's forming with all of this that I tell you, and the point is that (and he is showing me the rhinestones and the diamonds again) some things may look similar, but the composition and resonant frequency is different, as the internal composition is also different. Other races from other places may look the same but their bodily make up may be completely different from yours. Whilst some have the same properties, i.e. they can think, vocalize, and function in the world, they have entirely a different genetic makeup, not of human form at all. This relates back to the resonant frequency of the home planet, and your Earth fosters your type of human makeup, and is good for the human form.

Elaine: He is taking me somewhere now, to a big planet; and I can hear a huge, very slow booming noise. If you could imagine a 300 ft snowman or a giant just plodding along; boom, boom, very quietly, its like that. I can see that it looks like there is dark fog on this planet; it looks a bit like the swirling energy of those creature/beings that were together in the energy lake.

Ptplec is explaining to me that every time you hear this pulse or boom that comes up through the planet, it is organizing groups of molecules. It's like when for example; you spilled salt on the table, if you bang the table repeatedly, all the grains of salt group together or shift in the same direction. They all move together, and he's just trying to illustrate how things formed from a basis of sound and frequency;

and whichever sound was predominant, defined the type of being and defined the elements that would make up all the living things.

Ptplec: As I have told you before, all things attract energy into them. All things attract a soul or consciousness. Once the matter has formed, no matter if it is a lump of sodium, carbon, nitrogen, oxygen or hydrogen (which is what humans are basically made of) it attracts energy to *enliven it*…to give it life, and this is where the diversity of everything comes from. Things are formed according to the conditions created from within the host body of the planet by frequency, resonance and electro pulse. And as we have traveled the Galaxies searching for new things, we have found that we can determine the type of being that will be on any given planet, simply by detecting the signature frequency or melody of the planet, as it resonates into space; and sometimes we know that there will be life underground and not on the surface.

Elaine: He is giving me a visual of Europa which is one of the moons of Jupiter. It looks like a frozen planet, with lines all over it, and he is speaking about life under the surface of this planet.

Ptplec: We can detect a lot from a distance before we even approach somewhere, and we have an index of frequency to life form that we use as a guide when we are going anywhere.

Elaine: And he is asking me a question.

Ptplec: Why do you think I am telling you about all the different types of life forms that there are, made from as many different combinations that you could possibly think of?

Elaine: He is giving me a visual image of cookery, and is saying:

Ptplec: You can take a bag of flour, some water and an egg, and can make anything including pastry, soufflé, pancake or a cake with just those ingredients; altering the outcome by the addition of one more small thing, or by combining them together in a different way. With this example, I am trying to lift you and your perception of what you see around you, so that you can grasp the level of magnitude and miraculous concerning the diversity of living consciousness that there is in both physical and energy beings, and indeed, everything in our Universe.

You must look up from your one pointedness, and when I say *you*, I am talking about your whole race. Look up from your narrow beliefs that you have limits, and this is all there could be, or how could anyone function if they didn't breathe air, and that kind of thing, and look out at the Galaxy before you and acknowledge that *anything is possible, without limits.* And it all begins with light and dark matter. It all begins with that which reflects everything and that which absorbs everything. Do you understand? It is very important!

Elaine: Personally, I can't see why it is so very important to understand.

Reflection and absorption are two opposites, like a black hole ....and I was about to say a black hole that absorbs everything, but Ptplec is saying…NO…you have the theory of black holes, SO wrong!

But I am not going to go there right now, as I know we must come back to simple things like metal and crystals and similar.

Ptplec: I repeat, this is a metaphor for life…what you take in and what you reflect out go hand in hand together, and cannot be without each other. *Because that which absorbs, attracts energy, but within it is that which reflects, which gives back on an energetic level.*

Elaine: This is quite hard to grasp actually, because I have all these images in my head of vast crystals and big planet sized lumps of lead and things, and I know he is trying to make a really important point……I just have to keep calm and try to understand it! He is showing me a very interesting visual now. I am looking in my head at pictures of crystals that reflect, and also solid matter, like a heavy ball that absorbs.

Ptplec: Imagine something which absorbs, and goes on absorbing and absorbing and becomes heavier and heavier. Now imagine that which, like a hall of mirrors, receives light and reflects light.

Elaine: I see that the light that passes through things that are reflectors, goes *in and out*. He's showing me that it's like the difference between a saucepan and a colander. He saying 'imagine the saucepan is your dark rock and you're pouring water into it. Eventually your saucepan will become dense or so full of water that it can absorb no more. Now the colander has spaces in it which is like the light, and will always allow the light in, reflect it out, and allow it to pass through. Its always light, it's always working and it grows because of what it receives, and it will not be destroyed. It does not self destruct through over filling like the saucepan. I'm trying to put this into eloquent words....light does not self destruct, it always becomes more and in the process becomes more enhanced.

With this he's also giving me a metaphor for possessions...people having possessions......

Ptplec: You receive them in and to stay light, you must reflect them out. You let them go, you take what you need and you let them go. If you only take in and take in, your house will be so full up you cant get out the door, and what happens is destructive. For example, if you did that with a house....it would get hot, stuffy and cramped inside the house...say it was full of newspaper and crammed with 'things' it would get hot, it would rot or break down and then combust in the end.

And always within the dark matter there will be a core of light, because dark matter has this special quality. Dark matter will capture brilliant light and gather dark or heavy matter around it. When it gets to maximum capacity or density and it can't absorb any more, it begins to crack, break down implode, and the light must escape to go on again.

Elaine: Now I am not quite sure what the purpose of all this is,…this is probably Rule number one of the Universe, but I am just repeating what he is telling me, but I'm not sure I get it yet.

Ptplec: Don't you see? Everything mimics; everything is a mirror image, what you see outside, is what there is inside. I've just explained to you about matter solidification, and that everything has a light core inside. This is like human or physical existence also… when the human body cannot absorb any more, it cannot function any more, so it breaks down and out comes the light, which is your soul….out comes the energy.

I know this is a very …I wont say simplistic,….this is a very unsophisticated way to give you this but I am trying to illustrate that everything is, in a way, a mirror image of everything else.

We are all in this Universe, exactly like a fractal. You look, and you can see the whole design and if you home into one tiny piece, it's the same all over again' And the smaller and the deeper you go into the tiniest level of DNA, the concept, the pattern, the metaphor is exactly the same within your genetic makeup as it would be for the Universe.

And it works this way; for example, we'll go back to the hydrogen, nitrogen, carbon, and oxygen, the four basic building blocks of human tissue. You could take four other building blocks and create not another Earth human being, but another sentient being; and the patterning, or the fractal patterns would still be the same, just maybe instead of pink, they would be blue. If you just stand back and look at the whole of what I am speaking to you about, you will find the answer to so many of mans questions by looking outside; understanding the outside and knowing that what is outside the self, is also inside. I know it is difficult to make myself absolutely clear, but if you really think deeply on this for a while, you can connect to the concepts I was speaking about earlier on.

Think about why you are sometimes attracted to draw things to you; such as furniture, possessions, people, and situations. You feel attracted to go to a beach, a place or to see a person, and then at other times, you push away, you don't want it. It's a cycle within the self of need; its attraction of what is within, calling that which is outside. But if I said to you, you can also put that cycle on a planet, or on a Universe or on a Galaxy but think of it in huge terms…like sometimes a Galaxy will attract things, sometimes it will repel things, and there is an order to the consciousness of that whole Galaxy. It's not just a random thing; it is a need and a choice. I know this is very hard for you to understand; to think that lumps of rock, floating gas and miles of space, can be choosing or responding to an attractive thing. But it does!

Galaxies move towards one another because they are attracted. And that attraction can only be there in consciousness. Otherwise it would be static, nothing would happen; it would not be attracted or repelled, or it would not feel like absorbing or reflecting. And I am giving the word 'feelings' to it, because there is a lot you need to understand about the word 'feel'. We have spoken before about how to work towards mastering your emotions and your feelings, and how not to allow them to take control of you……that they are all there to serve you, but you need to be in a position of choice as to whether you feel you would like to be angry, or you feel you would like to be sad, it's the same with entire Galaxies of planets.

This is complex to try to explain; your definition of emotions is correct, but also incorrect, which as you know involves the law of paradox. There are always two sides to everything, such as absorb/reflect, negative/positive, and you have to understand that your emotions are the result of chemical interactions in the body, and electrical and energetic input from the mind, heart, and surroundings. There is hardly a distinction between the two when you reach a certain level.

They are one and the same thing because their interactions between one another are so simultaneous. It's a deep level I go into, but its all about the fusion of energy and matter which creates thought; and as both energy and matter has consciousness, the fusion of the two results in a translatable thought or idea.

Elaine: He is showing me again that all things….*all things,* everything, have the two elements of light and dark negative positive to them. He illustrates by showing me a long stick in my hand. On the one end you have everything that is light, and on the other end you have everything that is dark. When you get to the very mid point, light and dark become one….*its one thing.* But they are still paradoxically two things. They do not become one, they become like the Yin and Yang sign, they are both a whole thing but they are still separate. If you can understand that!

This is a **huge** principle here. You know, if you want to name the 10 principles that run the whole entire creation, this is one of them. It's difficult for me to grasp. I can repeat what he is saying, but there could be a million and one questions, and a million and one understandings. But the light of understanding could come on if you really thought about it…Phew!

And Ptplec is saying that we are just looking at page one! We are almost looking 'flat', and we still have to look up and down and sideways as well……but providing I can receive it, he is going to keep giving me examples until we get to a point where, we get a eureka moment, and we can see why, and see the meaning of it all.

Ptplec: Wherever you look, from a butterfly's wing or the wing of a Boeing 707 this principle is still the same. There are basic principles to matter, and *do not believe* that there is not consciousness in everything, because even a rock responds, even a creative machine. You know you speak sometimes about how you talk to your computers, cars or your washing machines to make them go; and on a simplistic level, you do have an effect on these things, but we must take this slowly enough to not either bore you or leave you in confusion.

Elaine (after session)…..I've just thought of a perfect example of attract and repel, even though its simple, and that is a magnet. You know one side is north and the other south…one attracts and one repels…..but what's in the middle? How can you attract and repel at the same time? What would you call that? We don't have a word for it, in fact we don't even *think* about it. If you could put all that in a movie…….I don't know how you would even portray it…I cant get my head around it…there are no words.

Steve: In a sense, you're talking about a feeling and it's difficult to imagine it, as it is limited by words and the fact that someone else is telling you. It's a massive shift in thinking, and to understand it you have to have the feeling and the experience. When you have that, it's incredibly easy and obvious. Whereas explaining with words is so apparently complex and difficult for me that I am furrowing my brow; whereas here (on the experiential side) it's a dreamy experience.

Elaine: Yes, I don't think you can figure this all out; you've got to feel it. Ok, imagine this: shut your eyes and imagine that you are this black heavy absorbing thing, like a black sponge at the deepest part of the ocean. Now switch and be a light, radiant thing, bouncing things off of you; a radiant with colour flowing thing, like a rainbow or a breeze from the ocean.

Now try to be the two things together. And that is impossible…how can you? I can't even begin to think how that would be…to be totally dark and heavy and absolutely light and formless at the same time. It has to be another level or dimension of thought…or it has to be only a feeling that can not be described by words.

Steve: Remember how we sat here a few weeks ago, and you said that what we were doing was the next stage of Eckhart Tolle's 'The Power of Now'? It's like being in those two states of Being and Doing at the same time; neither all one nor the other, but both at the same time. It's Doing from Being-ness, or taking action through stillness, and the only way to do that is to be *so* in the moment of now, and '*present*'. I feel this is almost the path, and yet that doesn't cover it somehow.

Elaine Yes, I agree.

Steve: Words just tie you in knots....and maybe that's what this session has been all about. Maybe you have to experience the 'knots' in your *head* in order to let go and get out of it, and that leads you into a space which is experiential in the *heart*.

Elaine: Yes. Instead of being either/or, you are both at once, the same as with being and doing, it becomes so second nature, you just *are*. And all of these wordy things are probably just leading us towards the state of being and state of mind that we have to be in. I.e. don't think about it, just DO it intuitively....that's the future!

They say that the human mind is a million times faster than a super computer at thinking (and computers are lightening fast); well this place is even beyond that. It's instant manifestation; like thinking a starship into existence. It's where you don't think about something anymore, you feel the desire for it ...and it is there. Because you are so aligned with the energy of BE and DO as one thing, it can't help but be attracted and manifest instantly.

Ptplec says that *energy must attract that which is solid*, as solid attracts energy. So when you are *being* that light energy within, and it's radiating off of you, all that you need in the solid material world MUST manifest. Bang! Like that.

I think this also applies to circumstances and situations too; such as when you need a lesson, you attract the situation or the person that will best teach you that lesson.

Elaine: And yet I can hear people saying oh yes?....what happens when you need a tin opener? Hahah! How is that going to manifest?

And I think the point really is….you probably won't NEED a tin opener! Because if you want a can to be open, it will be! Or you might not even need a can….you want a drink? Then there it is. So that sounds like it is EONS into the future for us…but maybe it's not as far away as we think it is? Because where we are right now is duality. You know, black or white, think or don't think, be or do.

I have heard all the 'New Age' people talk about coming out of duality and into oneness. Well maybe that's what this oneness is…..maybe everything is all together, we have to learn how to not be separate, or *think* of ourselves as being one thing or the other.

It's like mastering the emotions; if you become angry, that's like going down to the dark or black end of the stick; if you become hysterical with laughter, that's like going to the light end. Well it seems to me that you don't want to be at *either* end, you want to be balanced and steady with all of those things at your disposal, should you wish it. But you also want to be the *still* or ALL point in the middle of the magnet, where you neither repel nor attract only, but are repelling and attracting all the time simultaneously. You become all but cannot be defined as either…..Un-definable! Isn't that what the religions call God?

Steve: You cannot walk on the path until you become the path itself,

Elaine: I was going to say that's so hard to get your head around, but in a way, you can't get your head involved; it has to be your heart and your feelings. My mind says, well how can you know you're doing it if you don't think about it? It's a paradox and a conundrum.

Steve: Well, you know you're talking about feelings and the mind. And that's neither one thing nor the other

Elaine: Yes, it is all contained in the same thing inside-out and outside-in. When you take two opposite ends and combine them, it becomes a whole thing with everything in it; then you see the holographic third aspect of it. Remember when Ptplec talked about binary and energetic trinary code? It must be like that, which as far as I can see is all there is (for now, anyway!) In a way that's like God or the Creator, isn't it? No wonder some people say that we *are* God, and that God is within us and *is* us. Undefinable! When you combine anything physical, there is always the force, or the new energy of the combination. We could go on talking like this forever and get tangled in our own words, but it's so interesting!

Steve: Look at the opposites of everything and one thing. To understand everything, or to be at one with everything is to not be in 'nothingness', but in both places at once; to be individual and everything at the same time. Individuality is linked to possessions, needing, and ambition and the importance of thinking about what's coming next; but being in *this* moment now is full of potential, and in that, you can have everything. One of the things I am most interested in is being around nature, because nature has no ego, it just is what it is. For instance my big thing is being in my head, having ambition, which is like having control, which is like playing God, which brings me back to massive ego. In that cycle, I can't get to that point of 'now' presence when I'm in there…. because I am caught up in 'the dark'.

Elaine: But paradoxically you have to lose yourself in order to feel or find who you are, so you could go round in ever decreasing circles.

Steve: I keep coming back to John Lennon's thing, his line in a song was 'turn off your mind and float downstream'. Imagine the ease of that. I really believe that we know everything, we are everything, and at one will everything, but I can't get there by just believing it, I have to feel it.

Elaine: Yes, and Ptplec has said to me before: We have all the genetic material inside our systems to be anything that we want. It's just that we're at the stage in our lives where nothing is genetically turned on. In reality nothing is impossible, because we can turn on our other genetic codes by *being* in the frequency or feeling that activates or stimulates genetic codes into resonance.

Addendum:

Steve: What was Ptplec saying about your communication with someone a few weeks ago about trees walking around?

Elaine: Oh yes, I was at a seminar in the UK, and was talking to one of my colleagues, who on the one hand is an M.O.D chemist at the top of his field; well-respected with many people in his department, and on the other hand, he's a Reiki master within quite a few different disciplines. He is a lovely person who received a communication a few weeks ago that on some planets trees can get up or uproot themselves and walk around, then replant themselves in other places of their choice. And I happened to mention the same thing in passing as a kind of a joke really.

I said 'Oh, there is so much out there in the Universe, even down to trees that can get up and walk around' and he just clapped me on the back and said 'Oh, I'm so glad you said that, because it confirms what I was told by my guides a few weeks ago'.

Chapter 11.

Telepathic communication step one.

I am sitting with my 'receiver' (Steve) in session to speak to the Andromedans. At the moment all my guides are here, and I have called to Ptplec and Mir, but I can't see them anywhere.

They are just not coming, but what I do have is a very strong feeling here in my heart; it is a pulling feeling, it's almost as if the energy could come out of my heart to such a vast degree that it would turn me inside out.

I am now seeing a visual picture of lots and lots of diamond shapes with spaces in between. I don't know what that means; I've had no explanation for it as yet, but I have the feeling that I am meant to just be quiet for a moment, and feel something.

And now I have a visual of interaction with you, Steve, and I'm being told to say that you must put down your pen for a moment, and ask you to visualise a diamond shape here in your heart area; and then visualize a thick band of energy like a rope or tunnel from my heart to yours. I'm being told to just sit and experience it for a few moments. So I will turn off the tape and do that.

Heart links and telepathy.

So, now I will tell you what I'm seeing. Initially, I am seeing a visual picture that looked like a pupil of an eye, but it is actually representative of going through a circle and into a space. Then I saw circular waves of energy between us, passing from one heart to the other; then I felt and entered into amazing joy. It felt as if you picked me up as you would do a child, and swung me around. You were lifting me up, in a celebratory way, and I in turn felt like I was soothing you, stroking your hair and giving you lots of comfort, but also taking you by the hand and leading you to places in nature, like the woods perhaps. We were just like children would be, saying, come on! Let's go look and see what's in there; and we sat together and just reveled in the excitement and beauty of where we were; sitting by the water, looking out over the landscape.

What did you feel?

Steve: Well, I just sat, there weren't any visuals, but there was a really strong feeling in my heart of a tunnel; it had its own pressure, and it felt very strong and powerful, and it was good.

Elaine: That's wonderful…… so we both felt the energy!

Elaine: Okay, what I see now is a much smaller tube or tunnel going from my forehead to your forehead, and this one has colour to it, whereas the other one was like an open tunnel with circular wavebands coming round it. This is about the size of a neon tube, and it's a pale electric blue colour. It's so energetic it almost has sparks coming off of it.

I'm being asked by Ptplec to lock into that visual for the moment, as in mind to mind. My immediate feeling is that the energy here in the mind is like a flat desert plain, but it's also like Piccadilly Circus on a bad traffic day. There are a lot of thoughts rushing around; it's really difficult to describe or to give you example visuals, but I will try. I see all these thoughts rushing around like cars on the plain, and then they all sink underneath the ground, so that it is calm. I can now see the desert plain with miles and miles of nothing, and it is very beautiful.

Then I see lots of circular drain covers on the ground, and occasionally one cover would blow off and a thought (as a car) would pop up and start racing across the desert. Then other drain covers would blow up, and I see lots little thought-cars racing in all directions. Oh right, I think I am beginning to understand what this is about; it's almost like a visual guide to?.... aha!....I get it now, a visual guide to reading someone's thoughts.

I think Ptplec is here, but I can't see him yet; and he is telling me this is *Step number one in telepathic communication.*

Ptplec: We will go right back to basics; can you understand how the first scene I showed you was like traffic everywhere in the mind? There are thoughts just careering round each other, some thoughts collide with each other or back up behind each other and it's just like a traffic jam on the highway or gridlock in a city. You can see how difficult it would be, in a busy scene like this, to pull out or sort the 'thought-cars' into free flowing lanes of 'traffic'. Occasionally, you will see one 'thought-car' rise up above the others, but I have given you the visual of a flat plain with no cars on it as an example of what it's like when the mind is calm, and the person composed. This is a prerequisite for telepathy, i.e. for you to be in control of unwanted or random thoughts that clog up the mind. Once your control or calm state goes, that's when the 'drain covers' pop up, out comes a little thought-car, and off it goes racing in some random direction or other. When you are in a calm peaceful state, there is a clear field or plain in your mind, and one thought pops up, those thoughts can be easily identified. So having a clear calm mind but not with an 'empty head', is very important.

Elaine: Ptplec is now making a reference to us finding increasingly still points in our minds. They are the places where there is nothing in your head and you are just in a feeling of what is beautiful; he says that this is exactly the place to be for receiving and sending telepathic communication.

Ptplec: You already know how inspiration comes in when you can be daydreaming or even asleep. Whatever the calm state you might be in, suddenly an idea or a thought comes to you, which is just the right thing at the right time. This can be just like pulling out into traffic; if there is a huge traffic jam of thoughts in your mind, your marvelous idea cannot even get out onto the road! It has to have a clear space on the road in which to pop-up and drive on.

Elaine: I think this is a great example! Ptplec tells me to tell you Steve, that you have a great capacity for telepathic communication through feelings as well as thoughts, but your feelings are the stronger elements right now. And he says although you may feel at the moment that your heart and mind are separate, they are not as separate as you think. You have already integrated them quite well to a certain degree.

He also says, (and I know this is a funny area to go into), when you are without the body, (and I presume he means after you have died) you will have an immensely busy future in front of you with regards to communication, if of course it is your wish that you be of assistance in this way.

Ptplec: We know how inspired Steve is by people who endeavor with their creativity, and who struggle to release the diamond from within; and if he felt or knew that he could give them an extra blast of creative energy, or a lift that would inspire them to go on to be great people, I'm sure he would feel like he wanted to do it. As much as you love and enjoy this life, when it is finished and your time is over, there are even more fun things to do after that.

Steve: Brilliant!!

Ptplec: It is not by any chance that we suggested to Elaine that your home be the place of communication with us, and that you be the receiver, because this is all part of your personal journey.

Elaine: A bit of information has come to me in the area of your personal journey, Steve; Ptplec has just given me a visual picture of your mother.

Ptplec: Yesterday, we showed Elaine a brief telepathic visual of what was happening with her mother when she was at the Post Office; we can do the same thing for you.

Elaine: Briefly, to tell the story....I wanted to post a letter and there was nowhere to park. My mother was with me in the car (she is 88) and I left the car parked in front of someone's driveway, as I thought I would only be a few moments. When I got to the counter, there was a long queue, as there had been a post office worker strike and not many staff were there. As I was waiting, a sudden vision came to me of my mother being physically attacked through the car window by a man. At the time, I dismissed it as impossible and thought no more of it. When I eventually got outside, my mother was waiting at the curb side in distress, saying that the man who owned the house had come out and threatened her in a very angry way; he had said he would call the police and had really frightened her. As I got into the car, he came out again and was about to start abusing me verbally. I immediately said I was *so* sorry, and his anger melted away instantly! It was as if he couldn't think of what to say next....he suddenly looked quite blank, and backed away from the car. My mother was shocked at this, as she was expecting a huge argument with the man. I told her of my vision and realised that I should take much more notice of my telepathic impressions from now on!

To continue with advice for Steve and everyone with regards to telepathic communication from Ptplec:

Ptplec: Begin when in the company of the person you want to contact telepathically. Be consciously aware of staying calm, allowing the 'desert plain' or flat area in your mind that we spoke of before, to be clear and calm. You will notice when thoughts suddenly pop up, and you can do the heart energy connection exercise that we did before as well; because then you will be in communication with a totally different level of the other person.

The soul who came down to Earth to give you life and give you the situations you needed to learn from Steve, is your mother. You may find that by communicating telepathically, you gain a greater degree of understanding about how her soul fits with her persona as your mother. It will be most enlightening; you also learn more if you communicate telepathically with your brother. So if you have a quiet moment, just do that… You might find that you have an interesting experience—and we will help you with that, if you allow.

Ptplec: And now to more on the subject of telepathic communication. This is our first means of communication with the human race and it needs to be seriously developed. It's like learning any language; before two races can understand one another, they have to understand how the other works, and what their values are. So you can see how important it is that people on this earth learn how to receive and send telepathic communication. And of course we have chosen this time in your history because all the conditions are right.

As the Galaxies have moved though space, there have been changes in the atmosphere and the composition of energy which surround you on this planet; mainly from the 1960s, but even before in the 40s and 50s. And these changes have contributed to your steady progress towards your fourth dimensional seeing, viewing, feeling, and your opening to other dimensions of reality. And so in a way, we had to wait until you got to this stage before we could really begin to put our plans into action. Think back to the beginning of the last century, and you will find that people were already talking about 'life in the world unseen', the 'spirit world' and the 'other side'.

Now look out at the world today and see how attitudes have radically changed, and how many people are using their clairvoyant abilities;

how many people receive messages and trust their intuition. This ability curve is growing every day; you will see that within 20 or 30 years, your whole planet will be running mainly on feelings and intuition. People will be going against what is commonly known as 'logic' in order to follow their hearts. So in that way, you are developing and succeeding wonderfully in the right direction by yourselves. All we have done is come along at the right time in order to introduce you to the circumstances of the next decade or two, and to assist you with the next stage of your development.

Do you have a question?

Steve: No, not at the moment

Elaine: Steve, I am also told to remind you as well….. going back to the heart-to-heart exercise and the tunnels of energy.

Ptplec: Remember that distance is no object with telepathy, and that you could send telepathic heart energy now to any member of your family or any person anywhere, simply by sending that heart energy cord or tunnel out, to lock in to theirs. On a different level, your chakra energy is always linked together with those you are emotionally connected to, unless you have done conscious energy work to disengage it. You don't have to be close to someone in order to do it; such as being in the same room. We just give you a reminder here, and the obvious example is the distance we are away from you. It makes no difference at all; we can be millions of miles away and it is not a problem. In fact, I am millions of miles away. I am up on the ship right now and this is why you do not feel that my presence is in the room as you normally do.

Elaine: Yes, normally I can see and feel him quite close to me. But today I cannot see him at all, but I do get a visual picture of him now. I see him out there in space in a stationary starship, looking out of the window down at Earth. So *now* I can see him, and it's almost like he's waving to me from the window!

That's amazing! I find that really funny! (laughs).

Ptplec: Okay, these are simple steps illustrating that distance is no object, and that we are all connected in different ways. The more you learn about circles of energy, the better. I know you want to call them wormholes (pathways through the Galaxy in space), but in reality, they're not wormholes. You can call them that though because they are circular tubes that the energy passes through, and they look similar.

Elaine: So, I ask him now, what about the diamond shapes you showed me that are connected to the heart energy, what is that? If the connecting heart energy is a diamond shape, and now Ptplec is saying they are circles or tubes, I need an explanation here.

Ptplec is now telling me it has to do with mathematics. He is saying that the diamond shape, which is two triangles, one on top of the other, contains the circular energy cord that links heart to heart. The diamond shape is the container, and although I know absolutely nothing about mathematics, I probably need to look up and see if the sums of the edges are equal to the radius of the circle or something like that, and see how it fits together. But he says that the diamond is the perfect energetic shape to contain the energy of the heart.

Oh, and now he's taking me back to all those diamond shapes I saw at the beginning of this session.

These are the ones with all the spaces in between them, and what I see now is a diamond grid with lots of tubes of energy passing through them, the same as the tube of energy I saw connecting our hearts.

It's strange; I can see all the diamond shapes set up across the night sky, and they are quite small. I see diamond shapes, and diamond shaped spaces. But I know I haven't got the whole picture on this yet. I've just got a little piece of it.

Oh, this is funny; you know what a wooden clothes-horse is (for drying or airing clothes)? You can open it up, lock in the bottom rung, and it makes diamond shapes when it's open. Ptplec is showing me diamond shapes all around the earth or maybe in space around the earth. I'm not quite sure what these can be…..he says if you squeeze them together that's how you close them all (like the clothes-horse)… why….. I don't know.

He answers, when you close them all they become straight lines. It's a barrier of straight lines around the earth.

Okay; this is again very interesting. I am seeing all kinds of visuals on this.

I see an old fashioned television, and when I say old-fashioned, I mean from about 15 or 20 years ago, with a big heavy back on it.

Turn it sideways and you are looking at a kind of trumpet shape with a square front, (smaller at the back, bigger at the front). Now he is showing me a view from up on a starship, and I am seeing something extending from the ship. It looks like it's on a metallic arm, and it has a kind of sideways television shape with a rectangular front. It's like an old-fashioned Tannoy speaker. And now I'm looking down towards Earth, and all around Earth is this diamond mesh, with spaces and shapes, and he's telling me that this Tannoy shaped thing on the end of the metallic arm is used is to send frequencies to Earth; the frequencies are shot through the diamond shapes in order to contain them.

A 'sound laser' beam from the ship is split and passes through millions of diamond shapes to be contained; this is so it can be split and focused and has a precise destination. He says that this is how they are sending frequencies to specific people and places on the earth. I am getting the impression that what he has shown me is a very basic version of what is actually going on, and it's obviously much more refined than how I have described it.

Yes, this makes sense now, because he told me previously that they were sending frequencies to Earth; sending them to grid points and locking them into the electro magnetic grid around the Earth. I never thought about *how* they were sent, or what format they were sent in. I didn't know that there were millions of these diamond shapes around the earth being used to contain the frequencies and energy and to guide them somewhere specific. So I see that this is not just a random blast of frequency; it's a very focused project. It has huge intent and has been very carefully designed, like an architect would do; as everything has to be in exactly the right place for it to function properly.

Ptplec: We are very precise with content, structure and destination when it comes to something like this. This is also something for you to learn from with regards to telepathy. You need to be very focused, and for your intentions to have edges like diamonds, so that when you do this (practicing telepathic skills) you don't miss your target.

Elaine: He is giving me an example for you Steve, and that entails thinking about your mother. Imagine you have visualised her being in her kitchen. Now being in the kitchen is a huge space to be in, because it contains all the information about the kitchen and what it contains. So you first need to discount her physical shape and just visualise her energy, then 'see' her heart energy as your target, because it has to be very precise.

Now Ptplec is shifting to a visual of your brother and is saying, don't picture him standing there in his clothes, because you will have all the information about clothes, hair, shoes, etc to deal with as well. So first see him, then visualise his energy body, and then focus on the heart energy within the total energy field. This is a little lesson in being precise.

Elaine: Okay Ptplec, thank you.

At this point, he is giving me a mental list of points, and he says this should be included as steps for people to work with.

1. Finding yourself having a clear space like an empty desert in your mind

2. Allowing yourself to be in calm state of being.

3. Having the intention and the focus

4. Remembering that distance is no object

5. Knowing what it is you wish to communicate to, or feel from, the other person before you begin.

So for you Steve, there needs to be a reason; for example, if you wanted to find out if your mother was feeling happy right now, or if she was worried or sad; so you then go into her heart energy with a question… is there a feeling of happy, sad, worry, or any other emotion there, because Ptplec says that they have learned that communication is unnecessary unless there is a reason.

My human mind is coming in now and saying that you don't always have to have a reason to send love to someone……..and he is saying, well that *is* your reason, when you feel love for someone and you want to send it, that is your reason.

Elaine: I was a bit concerned there that that felt a bit like a very cold statement to make, but he is saying no no, no,….. *Really* think about what that means, and see how practical and useful it is to be uncluttered and in touch with your feelings. This is because reasons for doing things *always* come from feelings. Feelings translate into questions, such as 'How are you?'; and the reason is that you are concerned that the person you send your thoughts to is okay.

I know this all sounds really obvious, but he is really trying to break down every piece of this and say, *understand it!* The basis of any language or communication is learning the letters first, and then the words come, and then the language comes without thinking.

He also says he wants me to practice doing this, which is fun—and that over the next week, maybe I could practice with you. This is something everyone can do, and if you receive something that you sense is from someone you know, you can call or email that person, and tell them you felt it. So you can find out if you are open and sensitive enough to receive telepathy; even though all of our lives are so busy!

And so we will see.

Elaine: I have gone a bit blank here for a moment….and you remember the visual I had earlier on of Ptplec up in the ship waving to me? Well he has gone now, but his mother Mir has come forward now, and she asks if I would like to come up to the ship again. So I have said yes please, that would be wonderful; and I find myself now in the very soft corridors that I described last week. This time we are walking in the opposite direction; I have arrived at a window and it feels like I am going down the corridor to the right.

Mir says: We also need to teach you about how to use focused energy from the mind and heart to manipulate matter.

Elaine: She is talking about telekinesis! That's the moving of objects using the mind, or using energy from your hands to move something without actually touching it.

Mir is saying that Uri Geller has learned how to do this; how to manipulate energy and matter with his thoughts and intentions; and there are also other people in the world that can do it too. She tells me that it is possible for anyone to do, as it's a learned thing, like learning how to be telepathic.

The visual I am seeing on this (and again, its like a cartoon or a caricature of what it actually is)….is a red laser coming from the centre of my forehead or third eye area towards a pencil on a desk, and being able to move the pencil by thought.

Mir: We will back up a little bit to how you get to be able to do this. You have to be extremely focused, and in control of your mind. Your mind and thoughts must be peaceful, and not *trying* to do anything. It's a little bit like the martial arts masters on Earth when they want to break planks or bricks. They see the hand already *through* the bricks before they strike. So when trying to move a pencil, you see the pencil *already moved* and in the new place, as you do it. It takes a lot of understanding; some might call it faith or belief that it can be done. But let me assure you that it can be done, very easily. It's just a matter of focusing the right intention.

Steve: Can I ask a question?

Elaine: Yes please, ask a question.

Steve: It's about telekinesis. I always understood telekinesis to be something that's an exercise, like being able to move a pencil, but my thoughts are that it never really served any great purpose other than it being something mysterious and wonderful going on. Apart from that, it's an attribute that can be learned, it's a skill that is emblematic of something greater. So is there something that I am missing here with the importance you put on telekinesis?

Mir: The importance is that the ultimate object to move is **the self**. Compare this learning to when you attend a University, the end result of your study is the Master's Degree.

First is the understanding that utilizing energy for communication and transport *can* be done. Again, understand that we go in stages and steps; you first understand the energy, then fully accept and understand the power that you have. Then realize that you don't have to concentrate really hard; you don't have to be totally focused in *trying* to move things. It's approached from an entirely different angle. You approach from the knowledge that it is *already done*, and that needs to be learned, because you humans have a very strong logic that countermands your will and says, no it's not. *This is where you have to put in some major work with your mind, in order to allow this to happen easily.*

Elaine: Actually, I just lost my words then, because she showed me another visual picture of what I saw earlier on; it was me sitting in the woods with you, and this time I was levitating! I was sitting cross legged on the ground and I had levitated 3 inches off the floor! That's part of what this is all about, and *that's* the value of Telekinesis, because it's also linked in with defying gravity on our planet, and with manipulating energy in any direction.

So I'm thinking if you wanted to lift a heavy teapot off of a table up into the air, first you would have to deal with gravity, and then with what is linked to the teapot, like weight; then the resonant frequency of the teapot etc?

Mir: There are many aspects to anything that you can try to affect with your mind, and it's *not* something that you need to 'figure out'.

You can 'tune in' to the teapot mentally; your focus becomes *one* with the teapot, and from *within* the teapot, you affect it—the weight, balance and position. And therefore, that principle also applies to levitating the body.

When you wish to move, levitate, or go from one place to another, you are just considering mass or weight, frequency, the affect of gravity, direction and speed, and many other things, but this is not how it happens….it is more subtle than that. And so, as Ptplec has told you, as we begin to teach you about these things that you all can do, but will master in the future, they have to begin with baby steps, like moving the pencil.

Begin with learning to focus your energy from a calm platform or place where there is no other interference. It's like the 'laser' that came from the ship (which we gave you as an example), being split through all the diamonds, in order to reach specific sites. Without the focus, it would be totally ineffectual; it wouldn't work at all and would just be lost. So this is another step; all the things that we have mentioned today, from the heart to heart energy exercise between humans and the telepathy. *Its all about learning to be still and learning to be focused.*

Without having to *try* to quiet your mind, it's being able to drop or lower your brain waves instantly in order to calm them down from the continual sparking and rushing around that they do.

Elaine: She's giving me another example now. Imagine a thermometer with the mercury going up and down from zero to two hundred; this is like part of the output of our brain wave range. It's like a spectrograph voice print; but it's flashing in and out as it touches all the frequencies in different brain wave areas as you are using them.

Mir: In order to fire those brain waves up and make them work, there is an energy source within you, and when you sleep at night, at certain times your brain waves drop right down to around zero and below. Energy that is contained in the body builds overnight like a charge, which is why you do all your healing of the body at night; you rest and repair, you recharge. You have heard it said so many times.

If you can maintain a predominantly low brain wave state, as in delta and theta waves, i.e. a place of calm and focus whilst you are awake and alert, you are continuously building a charge within you *that can be used* to much more effect, like a laser. This is what you do in meditation; you go into theta and delta brainwaves. I am asking that you do it whilst being awake and alert; it's a *simultaneous* thing.

Mir: Because you are doing this whilst being awake, you can then focus consciously from a different level, and the power *to send and use the energy* becomes much stronger, because it's not being used up by being busy, busy in your mind all the time.

Elaine: This makes absolute sense to me!

Mir: It's an optimum and perfectly normal state to be in; to be able to function as usual in the world at this level, with calmer mind and predominantly lower brain waves. You will actually be much more effective than when there's a Piccadilly Circus traffic jam going on in your head!

As you begin to change, you will be amazed at how much synchronicity there is in your life and how easily that flows, until it just becomes a way of life and you won't think of it in any other way. You will also find that your tolerance for crowds, busy areas, electro-magnetic 'smog' will become a lot less...so this in turn will lead you into changes as a whole society of people. Changes in the way you build things, changes in the way you broadcast things. We are opening page one of a book that represents immense change to the whole world, and you have to take it page by page.

And already, over the last 30 or 40 years, people have been giving up life in the 'fast lane' (more in the western world of course) to go back to the countryside, to be themselves; to be creative artists and writers and find their joy, because people need the joy and clarity. Humans cannot function at such a fast pace continuously, as they have a tendency to leave the body and die early if they do. You shorten your lives and you create such illnesses when you are continually out of a state of calm. So we are here to say if you come back to that which we are teaching; the living from the calm place inside, the benefits of that are all the wonderful things we have been talking about, such as telepathy, levitation, and telekinesis.

You know, you all look at your lives and think, 'I must do something to reduce my stress!' That's just step one, yes, ok, we understand. In a way, you have *had* to go head first into the stress in order to understand that you don't like it, and that you can't function well in that state forever. So we are asking you if you would like to be totally 'chilled out' the whole time and be able to function at maximum capacity and form? This is what we are trying to point the way with. We are offering it to you so that you can say yes, and see how well it will really work.

Elaine: I am going to add something here from my own memory. I remember my mother saying to me …you wont get anywhere if you spend all day daydreaming; its the old paradigm from my mothers era, which was 'roll your sleeves up and get down to it, work all the hours God sends for a pittance and never have any time for yourself'.

Thankfully, this way of life is becoming obsolete, although you can still find that mentality in quite a few places…. So I sincerely hope from my heart that more people will begin to understand this message and know that we can still achieve a million things, but there is a different way to do it.

Mir says that this is enough now, as we need time to think about it, digest it and to practice all the previous things we have spoken about. To allow it to become as much a part of your life as a good breakfast, and to allow it to be as natural as breathing, and that's when life becomes effortless.

Okay, so I want to thank Mir very much for that information, and Ptplec for all that he has given to us, because its really nice to see it spelled out in plain language and to have a 'First plug in your machine' style step one to be able to share. Because lots of people, including me, miss the obvious, they don't think about it and don't really get the immense importance of it. I think Mir comes out with some really great truths in such a simple way. It's amazing.

Elaine: Going on to think about levitation…. Have you ever seen David Blaine on the television? Some of the things he does appear to be phenomenal, and somehow in my heart I just can't believe that it's a trick, especially the levitation. He could be walking along a street in London, with the cameras behind him, dressed in jeans and a T-shirt, with his trousers rolled up above his ankles. He might approach two strangers, stop them, and I think he always turns with his back to the people from about three or 4 feet away and then he just rises off the ground!

People's reaction is usually that of screaming and being amazed or astounded. There is definitely a least 4 or 5 inches between him and the pavement and I wonder how the hell he does it. And if it is faked, goodness only knows *how* he's doing it. He is the one that spent days encased in ice, and I sometimes think that he has to be an ET! He's got to be here to show people that we can do it…. what do you think?

I could be making an idiot of myself here, but whether or not these are illusions, I sincerely believe in what my ET Friends tell me. If you read Uri Geller's life story, you will see that in a way, he had to become a 'magician' in order to be accepted. But he does disclose that he had extraterrestrial contact as a child and believes that this is the source of his power.

Chapter 12.

07/07/2007

Another energetic point in the body

Identity and possessions.

It another Saturday afternoon and I am sitting in the warm glow of the summer sunshine. I've connected with all my guides and said hello.

I've just a comment here as a preface to what I'm going to say in a minute. There is one of my guides that I always call the 'Light Being' who always stands directly in front of me at about 12 o'clock position, and is always very radiant with light. As a change, I asked as I was going around the circle, 'Can you tell me more about who you are?' I then saw her side profile and I was surprised to see (I didn't realise this before) that she was one of the longheads or tall headed ET's. I know it is definitely a 'she' and interestingly I have seen these wonderful beings with other people, but didn't know that they were included in my circle of guides. She has always remained so shrouded in light, I never saw her this clearly before.

So now, I have welcomed in the Extra-Terrestrials, and I can see Mir the Andromedan female, and she's also brought her daughter today,… her other child.

Her daughter says her name is (sounds like) Andrieya. So now I have a name for her, which is good.

Then I also asked if there were any of my other ET friends there, and I see that my friend and guide from Sirius is there today, and also my ET friend from Lyra, who is very tall with long and slender arms, and has a luminous glow around him. The being that I know from Arcturus zoomed into my perception and then out again, just to acknowledge the fact that we are having a meeting.

Now the Andromedan 'Mir', is nudging me to focus my attention on the middle of my body, which is where my waistline would be, in between my naval and solar plexus. She's talking about things which are in deep, and I'm drawing back from the conversation and looking at that area of the body, and the words she is saying are ' in depth'.

So, I'll just check and see what she means by this. Aha! Right, I understand.

Mir: We have spoken in the past about the brain and the mind; we have spoken about the heart area, and now I want to go to the area here, around the naval, the middle of the body, and speak to you about its connections to the Earth and family.

Elaine: I was going to add here that this area is sometimes known as the Hara by martial arts people. But I am corrected, because the area she is referring to is slightly higher, and really on the waistline. She is giving me a visual of being connected to my mother with an umbilical cord, but I'm also looking right through the body from that point to the spine, just where the spine joins with the pelvis.

She is saying that this is also an important point in the body, because this is the area where we store all things, such as emotions, and earthly things that keep us anchored to everything that is here. This is interesting because we were just talking earlier about me and my possessions, and my need to sort through and get rid of all the excessive 'stuff' I have collected over time.

I find it fascinating to compare to you, Steve, because you find that getting rid of your possessions is extremely easy, and I find it very difficult. So I am going to be quiet and stop talking now, and ask Mir what it is that she wants to say.

Mir: All the things that you humans fight about and get stressed with are all those things pertaining to the 'I', or the self; the 'I' you recognize as who you are when you look in the mirror. And the 'I' that you recognize in Earth terms needs identification; needs an identity which is apart from who we are in the *outside* world; that being maybe someone's boss or a garage owner or a bus conductor.

But the 'I' within the personal world need mirrors within the things that are around it to reflect the self back to you. Now when I say mirrors, I don't mean the real mirrors that you look in to brush your hair. I mean, when Elaine looks at her medical books, and her art books, and finds it so hard to let go of them. There is self identification when you look at something like that that says, yes, that's part of me. Yes, that's something I love, and something I identify with, and it's something I wish I was, or is part of me.

Elaine: For me, I don't necessarily wish that I had been a doctor, but if I had been a doctor, I would be in a much better position than I am now in order to help people with their health problems, in terms of Earth qualifications and prestige. And also when it comes to being an artist; had I taken the place offered to me in Art college and got myself a degree in art, then I think I would carry much more weight, and be more 'saleable' in the art world within the structure of expectations that people have about what is art, and who artists are. And so I see that those things, those art and medical books, give me a sense of security and identification; a 'let's not forget that this is part of you' feeling, which is why I find it so hard to let go of them.

Mir: The same applies with music, and the musical instruments that you love, and so on. It's because part of you would have loved to have been a musician on a grander scale, rather than on a small scale. All these things are mirrors that reflect back to you, and are like cushions around you; they support you in maintaining your sense of identity, reminding you who you are and where you fit into society. And they resonate not necessarily in the mind, but that is where they might end up; they resonate here at the waistline in between the bottom of the stomach and the naval, simply because this is your anchor pin to your credibility on earth. I suppose you could call it the solar plexus, but it is a bit lower than that. This is also where you store your images of how you think other people see you, and how that matches to the self image you have created inside.

Elaine: (Again, this is a topic we were talking about earlier)

Mir: This is commonly why, when you are upset, the feeling in the 'stomach' and the digestion is very acute, and sometimes you can feel very sick, and you need to go to the bathroom or toilet. This happens when something upsets you on a very personal, 'who am I' level. And if we are to be detached from this storehouse of imagined perception of the self, then we need to pull the plug (as it were) and lose our sense of identity. This is a step towards not being one thing, but being all things.

When I say, 'lose your sense of identity' that, in human terms, comes across as very scary or frightening; because unless you know who you are, things can get difficult in the world. Do not mistake what I say for lack of self esteem, self worth or identity. I want you to look at this in a *finer* way and say to yourself; it is a transition from self imposed limits to unlimited-ness. First you let go of your concepts of who you think you are, and this for Elaine will make letting go of all her paraphernalia, her mirrors, much easier. But it then comes full circle to the next level, so that you understand that you are *all the things* only more so, *Everything.*

So, instead of wanting to have been a doctor, or wanting to have been a 'qualified' artist with a degree, or a botanist or chemist (and I know

Elaine has all these desires inside of her); lose that identification with what represents those things on earth.

For example; the concept that you must have a whole bucketful of qualifications and study in order to *be someone.*

You can step out of that into the knowing that we are all botanists, chemists and artists and that we are all part of everything. Take off the labels, cover up those mirrors that give you back earthly conceptual reflections, and then allow a more universal 'dome' over the top of you to be the thing that reflects back to you which is: *you are nothing but you are also all things.* And when I say nothing, I do not mean inconsequential, I mean, you are without Earthly identification, *a slot.* Come out of your BOX, the slot that you put yourself in, and become MORE. As I have said before, this is a step towards loosening up the energy in this area that keeps you very much anchored to concepts and possessions.

Take someone like your friend Steve, who has slowly been shedding all the mirrors around him; has few possessions, and whose identification now is really only as a creative person. His chosen path was within the realm of music, and now it's within the realm of film, and even that is identification.

Steve, you are creator of mood and expression, a creator of subtle inference. If you can step into the 'I am nothing' (and that doesn't mean you don't amount to anything, it does not have earth connotations; rather it means I am identity free); after having experienced that place, you will find that your life path is leading you towards stepping into a place of 'I am all things'.

For example, it's like having total amnesia. If you had total amnesia and didn't know that you could play the piano, or didn't know that you could create beautiful films, not only would you rediscover what you *can* do, you would also re-discover what you don't know you can do now. This area of the body that we speak about obviously connects directly to the brain. It contains the way we think and view the world, the seeing of colours; everything that relates to the inner self, in fact. It is a genetically inherent tendency that you learn who you are from reflected outside sources right from the beginning of your life, even including whether you are male or female.

Elaine: Okay, I understand what Mir has said so far, and I ask her the question: what do we actually do with this? How do we achieve this thing…. when you say, 'pull the plug out'. What do you really mean, in practical terms?

This is very interesting; as an answer, she has just come up with another concept from me to look at.

She is showing me a visual of myself with a blindfold on and saying:

Mir: Imagine if you were blind and had no concept of what you looked like, and you could not see what it was you were eating when it was in front of you. Every sensation, smell and taste would be different, and your analysis of what was happening around you would be coming from a different place too.

It wouldn't be coming from *here* in the stomach area, it would be coming from your finer senses, such as your subtle sense of smell and your heart *feeling*. You would ask yourself, how does it feel? Do I feel good today? You would not say 'do I *look* good? Let's look in the mirror. You would say, 'Do I *feel* good and do I *feel* comfortable? What do I really want?

If you are not using your sight to identify things such as cake, biscuits or pork chops, pink cardigans, or shiny shoes….. which are all about 'how do I *look* to others' and what do I *think* I want….. Then it comes down to *how do I feel about myself and what do I feel I need to eat*?

If it were a pair of shoes the difference would be not, 'are these the latest fashion', but 'do these feel comfortable and kind to my feet'? Do they feel like they belong to me? When it comes to food you would be very much more in touch with your body. You would ask internally, does my body need or want something sweet, something with vitamin C in it, or something with protein?

If you referred to your feelings within all these areas…. not just sight and smell, but also taste and hearing and touch, all things which are truly what you need or want would be much more easily accessible.

Elaine: This is a really good example to illustrate what she has been talking about. The whole point is about whether you focus your attention outside the self, or you focus your attention inside.

I allowed myself to be distracted just then by a noise outside and I opened my eyes, and it was like pulling the plug out of my connection to her. To be truthful, I think she (Mir) has done this purposely; because if I was in a 'reading' with someone I can do that easily… I can open my eyes, close them again and go back to where I was in the reading.

It's usually not a problem for me, which is why I did it just then. But maybe she has given me this as an example of pulling the plug out or pulling the connection out to accessing so much more with their eyes closed. Of course we need to be able to do it with our eyes open eventually, but that whole flow of information from her is gone now, once I became occupied with the distraction outside.

I see it now; it's almost like when you are distracted by things around you, *that* is when you are blind. That's when you can't see, when your eyes are open, because of all the visual distractions, and because you are turning off your sensory perception in order to allow visual input. When you visually take in so many frames per second, all that data diverts you away from what you should be *sensing*.

This has all happened at exactly 7 o'clock on the 7th July 2007 and I wonder if there is any significance in that, or whether there is some kind of planetary thing going on! I do find it phenomenal that my connection was closed so abruptly in the middle of receiving messages from Mir; and when I looked at my watch, it was exactly 7 o'clock. So I can only guess at the meaning, but as a lesson, it did make an impact! Very strange!!

Chapter 13.

Awareness and Consciousness

Well, it's a bit like crowded house today...guides and spirit friends and family everywhere including members of your family Steve, and my family too. Everybody is grinning very broadly, and they are all really pleased that I am now in the position I am in, which is much freer from commitment than I was.

When my guide the Light Being came in, she pointed a finger at Steve and one at me and made the triangle between her, my heart, and his heart, and is just reminding me that we are always connected.

I have invited the ET's in, and Mir is there along with Ptplec and his younger sister. Ptplec has said that he is going to give me an 'in conclusion' or an addendum to the things that we have already got down on tape, and he wants to remind me that the two words, *awareness* and *consciousness* are probably two of the most important words that there are within our language today.

Ptplec: One word means knowing- which is consciousness, and the other is acknowledging the knowing, which is awareness. The obvious key to stepping forward in all things is first knowing that *everything* is conscious, and then allowing yourself to become fully *aware* of it.

Fully aware are almost 'throw away' words that pass people by very easily, until you look at the bigger meaning of 'fully aware', as this means fully aware on *all dimensions*.

Elaine: I think if we were fully aware on all dimensions we would probably be so expanded we would disappear!

Ptplec: Please don't dismiss this as being unattainable. It is very attainable, and you are on the path towards getting there as we speak, but it is something that needs constant vigilance and attention, because the important thing about attention is this. If you don't have your attention on your awareness then your awareness melts into the background, and you become unaware, which is the same as being in the dark.

Elaine: He is just reminding me that there is no place anywhere within our known universe that you cannot go to when you use your awareness and consciousness together, and can direct them.

Ptplec: Everything is open to exploration, including the development of your solar system and the changing nature of the planets in and around it. You call this kind of thing remote viewing; we call it mental teleportation with all your senses turned up to the max. That obviously means your five physical senses, and also those beyond that. Every physical sense has its energy counterpart.

For you all, the external discovery and exploration of new things that are outside of the self is a wonderful ongoing project; but what of TODAY what of NOW? What of the journey within the self that is happening every second of every moment in the now? In order to fully understand the journey within and inside the self, you have to understand that the physical body combined with the energy body is the conduit to within the self. It's also the conduit and lens that you look through to go out of the self. So the more accustomed you are to seeing through the lens which is yourself, the better you will be at seeing what else is out there.

Elaine: He's giving me a really strange and odd example of an exercise that's good to do, and that is 'seeing' with every part of your body.

Ptplec: We have spoken about extra internal sight, but imagine how it would be if your eyes were situated on the ends of your toes? Imagine if your nose was on the end of your toes; being able to smell or sense things at ground level for example. You know on average you spend most of your life smelling things that are at five or six feet up in the air?

And he's pulling it from my mind a story I heard a couple of days ago about a 12 year old boy that can detect truffles under the ground with his feet, and apparently he is making an absolute fortune for his father because truffles are worth thousands of pounds per kilo!

This boy can feel through the ground with his feet, and without looking, can find where the truffles are. Usually truffles are found by pigs, and pigs use their highly developed sense of smell; so what is he doing? Maybe he is sensing and smelling, searching and seeing through his feet?

He must have turned up his 'awareness' to a huge degree and perhaps is tuning into the earth and the third dimension? Vibrating with the Earth itself and to the energy and frequency of the truffles?

Ptplec: I am here to remind you that you cannot do anything better on a daily basis than to 'turn up the volume' on your awareness. Pump up the volume on the extra sensory perceptions that fit together with your sight, hearing, taste, smell and touch. This is like doing exercises everyday, flexing your sensing abilities to keep these things well tuned and well honed. *Because being in tune and sensitive to the elements are the first steps to being able to absorb the energy from the sun, the air, from the atmosphere around you, in order to sustain life on a totally different level to that which you are accustomed.*

If for example there was no food after tomorrow, and you had only water, the human race would either die or have to quickly adapt to taking its energy from elsewhere. You have seen some of your gurus or yogis (as you call them) live on very little food, and still maintain their life or aliveness simply by pulling in the energy that is all around them.

In a way, we do not wish that you as humans become necessarily like us, but that you go to a *better* place than we have evolved to. This is because we have developed our bodies and adapted to very different kinds of food from that which you eat; we consume a lot less, and we have mastered our emotions; but there are rare qualities of humanness that we admire we love very much. Your ability to sing with such beauty; your ability to physically express your passions, whether it be music, physical union, a joy of living or swimming; these are qualities that our race admire. I was going to say that we 'long to experience' with the freedom that you do, but that is not to say that we don't swim and we don't have union; we do have energetic union; but within that there is an element which I am finding it particularly difficult to pinpoint, as I am using Elaine's mind.

Elaine: Because Ptplec is switching backwards and forwards from our existence to his existence, he is also trying to allow me to feel what it is he really means.

It's an essence of such subtle complexity it is difficult to say. We humans are trying to extend our senses out to the energetic equivalent of sight, sound, hearing, touch and so on. The Andromedans already possess that information within their energetic senses, but they would appreciate having a slice or a colouring of the physical sensations and the things that go with our essential humanness…..

Ptplec is trying to let me feel that they would like to add human 'play' as a colour to their palette (and I am really explaining this badly) whilst still retaining their uniqueness, obviously. So when he says to me that the Andromedans would like us to attain all that they have *and* bring our own essence with it and not lose it, I can understand what he means.

But he says when any pendulum swings you have to go to the extreme opposites before you come back into the middle with equal balance and perfect harmony between the two ends. Now I can visually 'see' what he is trying to say, and is simple.

Because the human experience is such a unique and wonderful thing, we should be wise enough not to progress so rapidly into the future that we lose that which we would regret losing later.

Elaine: It's like the difference between analog and digital music, there is no substitute for a hearing an instrument like a saxophone play live, because within the performance is the whole energy of the player and the instrument itself blended together; there is so much more emotional information in the performance package, and it's richer with this emotional energy. Digital recordings are more bright and brilliant, but the higher and lower harmonics are cut off and lost for the sake of digital clarity.

Mir's daughter.

Mir's daughter has stepped forward now…. and she has a totally different energy to Ptplec. Her energy is very soft and warm and steeped in such a feeling of love, that it's quite an experience to connect with her.

Ptplec's energy is very bright and vibrant; exciting, clear and informative; whereas her energy is like it would be if you closed your eyes and could smell a rose, could touch it to your lips or skin, so perfumed, so coloured, and so soft.

And she speaks about the united hope of the ET races…. hope for the best and most fruitful outcome of their interaction with our planet.

She is allowing me into her heart space, and I can feel the tremendous love that they have for all things living, all things conscious. Not just humanity, not just the human population, but for every single thing, every single miracle that grows and is on the Earth.

There is this immense feeling of awe, gratitude and connection to every living thing. I can see her eyes again now, and she says this is the prime reason we come; we risk rejection from you; we hope that our careful plans to introduce ourselves slowly enough will not be fruitless; because it's like seeing a beautiful rose bush in the path of a digger. And if you will not allow us to come and transport you out of that space to another place (and I speak metaphorically), the digger which is bent on your destruction, could overwhelm you.

When I say this, I am not speaking in terms of 'your planet is going to blow up and everything is going to be destroyed and you will be dead'. That is *not* what I mean.

What I mean is, that we hope against all hope that you accept us and allow us to give you the protection and teaching that you need; because in reality, the metaphorical rose bush which is you all and your planet, still remains and grows in the same spot, it's just that with our help and the help of many other ET races, it will move to another higher dimension, so that it cannot be touched by the 'digger'.

On Earth, you have no real inkling of the amount of change that will happen within the next 50 years. Your planet is undergoing huge climactic changes which will alter the landscape and alter the populace; and we will be there for you. When we spoke in the very first session of the Earth being like a garden, and picking the flowers (people) to take to our ships, we speak not in metaphor but in truth. There will be many occasions in which we will need to remove people temporarily from the Earth and place them down somewhere else. And in that one sentence, the implications are huge for physical and mental trauma within humans, and I cannot express to you enough how important and urgent it is, that our contact become globally much more real and accepted. Not just accepted by isolated pockets of people, we must be known to *all* people.

Once that has happened, and it is a delicate thing, because we spoke earlier of our hope of not being rejected; as far as our reception goes, we know that the majority of people will accept us and our aid. Who might *not* accept are such governments who rule with military power, using fear.

And so our operation is delicate,... and we are using all the power that we have with mental telepathy to allow people to understand about us unconsciously, even if they do not accept us consciously at this time. So when the time comes, it will seem as if you knew all along, and it is perfectly normal.

Elaine: As I am speaking her words, I am feeling this is *so much* from her heart, so from a place of *'please accept us'*; I feel open hands, open minds and open hearts. Without question, when you connect with ET's like this, you can really feel and know what their agenda is.

Without any shadow of a doubt, I know that the Andromedans are really coming from a place of love; especially the ones that I am in communication with, who feel like they are better than a best friend to me. It's as if they have known us all our lives and they are here to take our hands when we need it. So it is enlightening and heartening to feel the energy behind their motivation and their concern for us.

Steve: Can I say something?

Elaine: Yes, please do.

Steve: There is one thing I want to say before I ask a question, and it is that *I feel her energy so strongly in the room. It's really physical. It's the energy of love, passion and vision and unconditional love involved with her wish.*

And my question is…. can you ask her what her name means?

Elaine: Yes….. She tells me that the name she gave last week which was 'Andrieya' is a humanised form of her real name. Her full name is actually much longer and means 'Woman of Andromeda'. She says that in the same way that you call my brother Ptplec, and his name is a lot more complex than that; this naming serves the purpose that we need it for.

Andrieya is taking me forward a little bit into the future now, to when I go to meet the Sasquatch (Bigfoot) in October, and she asks me.

'Will you take *our* message to the Sasquatch personally?'

When she says that, I know that she knows the Sasquatch people are in contact with Extra-terrestrials; but she wants me to take this very personal feeling that comes from their family; link up with them, and give them the exact emotion that I felt from her just now.

Andrieya: When they feel our love, it will bring them much closer to you; there will be a great deal more understanding, and it will encourage the Sasquatch people to come forward and be a bit more open with you than they have been previously. It's an energetic exchange, and when that passes between you, it will build another step on the bridge between you and them.

The Andromedan 'father' of Ptplec and Andrieya.

Elaine: Wow, this is interesting! I am now being introduced to Mir's male counterpart who is the 'father' of Ptplec and Andrieya.

Father in our Earth terms is a slightly incorrect word, but needless to say, together they created these two children. He is taller than Mir, which makes him about 7 feet six; and he has a very different energy feel to him.

I can feel his disposition, and I will describe it; he is a 'man' of great strength and wisdom, I see his energy like a steel pillar inside him, glowing and sparkling with an electrical field around it; he has great inner strength and ability, and he is honoring me by allowing me into his mind. I can see energy and focus of attention coming out from his mind in twelve different directions at once; (and we think we do multitasking here on earth?)!

I shall describe it. Imagine a band around your forehead like a circlet or crown. From his head area at this point comes twelve beams of light, radiating out in twelve different directions all around his head.

He is splitting his awareness into all twelve places at once, and giving each portion of awareness his individual attention .... like a master of.......*a master*. How else can I put it really?

I have never seen anything like this; Mir has not shown me this kind of thing before. Maybe it's another level of energetic mastery? Oh boy, I can see that whilst we are aspiring go out on *one* beam of light and put ourselves somewhere else, he is doing it in twelve different directions at once!

And despite the fact that I likened him to a steel pillar with energy all around it, he is allowing me to see that he actually has a very good sense of humour; and that his 'inner child', or the childlike qualities within him are quite strong.

I can feel that he finds amusement in everything, simply because he is in a state of happiness, I suppose you would call it, all the time.

So, I am looking at layers here,.... this kind of solid steel core, with all this energy swirling around him but a great sense of humour and a brilliant mind; and an ability to control energy like I've never seen before.

But warm with it as well……. It's no wonder that Mir chose him, or rather, they chose each other.

They are partners in order to bring forth children; and I can feel very strongly the kind of things that he is involved in at a higher level. He is involved in teaching, but also in negotiation in arbitration, in decision-making; everything to do with making bridges between the other races and us on the earth; but not on such a personal level as Mir is with Earth people.

He is showing me that he can manipulate energy with his hands. He can project his thoughts and make them manifest as a hologram in front of him. So for example, he is holding out his hand, and suddenly I see a perfect replica of the Earth floating in space above his hand. He's telling me that he is sending this mental image to the space above his hand then holding a column of energy from his hand, so that when the two energies meet, the Earth appears.

That is; the telepathy from his mind and the energy from his hand are like two lasers meeting, and coming together. The energy from his hands is flowing from his heart, where the *feeling* of the Earth is; and when combined with the mental image from his mind, you get a holographic image of whatever it is he is transmitting.

So in simple terms, what I see is a replica of the Earth, and I am told that he can show all kinds of messages in this way.

But that seems to me to be one stage beyond *just* telepathy. The more I am experiencing and learning about telepathy, the more I am realizing that you don't hear just hear the transmitted words. There is much more to it than that, and the message in words is only one dimension of it. He is showing me that you hear the words and feel the feelings, and that the feelings colour the words immensely.

The words are for my benefit of understanding; the feelings are much more important. Then the next stage beyond that is to manifest those energetic thought forms as a holographic image.

And together as a group, they tell me that there will be many more things they have to tell me as time goes on; but what is of prime importance is the information that we have already gathered right now. It's important that it's put together as quickly as possible and dispersed, and I hope they will help me to be guided to the right places to go, because even in its raw form, the information here is really important.

So they are saying that there is no more to say now; the bite that we've got to chew on is sufficient up to this moment in time, because we are in the middle of everything on Earth, and it's important that people understand what the next step will mean and be ready to evolve. And people need to be open and ready, because if they do experience lift off on an ET ship it will be for a very good reason. There's nothing to fear at all.

Steve: Can I ask one last question? I'd like to know his name…. Mir's partner……. the father of the children.

Elaine: Okay, yes, I will ask.

Uh oh… so now he is giving me the full nine yards of his name, which is more like a sound. For my ease of understanding, he is condensing it into human alphabet letters, so that I can get it. I will spell it as I can see it.

PTLAMGANENON…… and he says stop there because that's enough! It's sort of pronounced Lam-gan-non, or almost like that. But when he says it and I feel it, it has a metallic sound in it. It has a musical note in it that you couldn't reproduce if you tried; not with your mouth anyway.

It represents tensile strength; and it's funny but he is saying we are named with qualities, essence, feelings…. our language is a visual, pictorial, feeling language, which when spoken contains much more than just verbal sound.

It's a tough one to get your head around really. Mir is a shortened version of the female's name, but there is a real feeling of simplicity and openness to it; of flexibility and kindness, and it really epitomises her energy. She has a kind of grace that is beautiful to feel and very loving. So, I am just going to give them my personal thanks, and my promise that I will get off my butt and do this now. :o)

END

7/2/2705

Happy Spring
grandma

door / Garden w/table
flowers
people

Made in the USA
Lexington, KY
15 November 2010